The Beekeeper's Guide

The Beekeeper's Guide

Guide

Fun and Simple Steps to Apiary Success and Self Sufficiency

Trevor Darby

Urban Homestead Books

Salt Lake City, UT

For information about permissions to reproduce
selections
from this book, write to Permissions, Urban Homestead
Books,
1352 West 7800 South, West Jordan, UT 84095

Library of Congress Cataloging-in-Publications Data is
available.
ISBN: 978-0990806905

For Camylle

my queen bee

Contents

Thank you for purchasing this book.

If you absolutely love the idea of producing your very own delicious honey but have no idea how to get started, this is the perfect book for you. If you want to create a sustainable source of healthy food for your family, this book is for you. If you are hoping to build a viable business that provides for your family, this book is for you. If you just love bees and are fascinated by their fuzzy little bodies and their happy buzzing sounds, this book is for you.

Beekeeping can be fun as well as profitable. Local grown honey often sells for between $5 and $7 a pound. With a typical hive able to easily produce between 50 and 100 pounds of honey per year, this can mean a serious boost to your household income or even a full time job if you want to grow your new hobby into a business. Perhaps you just want the security of knowing you have a ready source of nutritious food available to you and your family no matter what happens.

Beekeeping as a hobby is enjoyed by over 200,000 people in

the United States and several tens of thousands more throughout the world. Human's fascination with bees has been going on since the beginning of recorded history. With a little advice and guidance, you can become part of this noble tradition. Getting started in beekeeping is easy to do. Once you know the right steps to take, it will be a rewarding hobby that provides healthy food for your family, loved ones and friends.

When I first started beekeeping nearly a decade ago, I had no resource to teach me the steps. I went to the local bee shop but wasn't able to understand a word they said. So I went to the library and my local bookstore and found every book I could to learn the art of beekeeping. After thousands of pages read, hundreds of hours spent practicing beekeeping, and many chances to share the skill and benefits of beekeeping with several hundred people, I have learned a few things I want to share with you.

First, beekeeping is a joyful, simple and soulful activity. Second, getting started is very easy if you have the right information and training. My goal with this book is to give you the information and training you need to get started keeping bees with minimal fuss and bother and to share with you the joy I have found in beekeeping. This book will teach you everything you need to know to get started keeping bees. From there, you can provide honey for your family and friends, produce wax for candles, salves, and soap, or even build a profitable business keeping bees.

So, without further ado, turn the page and let's take our first flight into the world of the honeybee.

Trevor

Introduction

This book is laid out to be read from beginning to end. It is divided into five sections. The first section is All About Bees. In this section, you will find answers to many questions about bees, their homes, as well as their activities. The second section is Get Ready, Get Set, Go. In this section you will find the information you need about gear, hive placement, and choosing between different strains of bees. This is the planning section. By the end of this section, you should have everything in place to welcome your first hive. The third section is Settling In. Here you learn how to install your hive into their new home, how to care for them, and what things you should be on the lookout for. The section continues with the proper steps for summer care of your new hive. The fourth section, Harvest and Beyond, is all about getting your honey from the hive into your kitchen. It details what steps you can take to prepare your hive for winter and into the second year. The fourth section ends with a discussion about problems that can arise in your hive and what to watch out for. Then the fifth and final section, Fun Beetivities, goes through all kinds of fun things you can do with your hive produce. The chapters are set up so you can refer back to them often and find answers to questions that may come up as you are working with your bees. I hope you find as much joy from your bees as I find from mine. Before we jump into All About Bees, let's talk about a couple of things that are probably on your mind.

It is important that you consider a few questions before you get started beekeeping. First, are you, or is someone in your household allergic? If you are truly allergic to bee stings, you need to move on to another hobby.

Second, do you have space for at least one hive? A hive will travel up to a mile and a half radius to collect food, so you can keep bees even in the middle of a city. The bees will find flowers and trees all on their own. But you need to have a few square feet to actually locate the hive. You can do it in nearly any size backyard.

Third, is it legal in your area? Check your local city laws and state laws with a couple of quick phone calls before you spend money on equipment. Depending on your city and state, there may be a licensing fee to keep bees. This is to help pay for the bee inspectors in your area. Also, if you are going to keep bees, it may be something you want to discuss with your neighbors, even if it is legal in your area. Most neighbors will be delighted and won't care at all, but they will appreciate it if you talk with them first. Be a good neighbor.

Fourth, are you willing to spend the time to do it right? My parents always taught me if I was going to do something, I should do it right. You can expect to spend anywhere between 10 and 40 hours a year to take care of one hive. Most of that time is during the early spring and late summer. If you decide to have more than one hive, you take advantage of some economies of scale. When I had just four hives, I would typically only spend about 25 to 40 hours a year working on my hives. The majority of that time, about 20 hours of it, was split between early spring and then the harvest in September. Beekeeping on a small scale requires just a modest investment of time; but once you start, it is important you spend the time so you and your bees will have a happy, healthy, and successful relationship full of sweet rewards.

Fifth, do you have the money to get started? To get started is going to cost somewhere between $200 and $500 depending on how serious you are about the beekeeping hobby.

If you are comfortable with your answers to this question,

and you have an interest in beekeeping, then by all means—get

beekeeping. Read on to learn how.

All About Bees

The Beautiful Honeybee

The humble honeybee has been providing food for humans for several thousand years. Humans have long sought out this tasty source of energy packed with vitamins and minerals. It not only provides basic calories, but also delivers much needed health benefits.

The honeybee lives in a hive. The hive structure is simple, yet breathtaking in its beauty. A wild hive can nest inside a tree, a cave, in a deep dark crevice or even in the attics or sides of buildings. Bees prefer to make their homes in protected areas so they are safe from bad weather and predators. A wild beehive consists of several lobes of honeycomb that provide a secure and sanitary area for the bees to raise their young and store their food. Sounds kind of like people behavior to me. Honeycomb is built of many tiny hexagonal cells that function as storage spaces for honey and pollen. The honeycomb also serves as birthing chambers for the bee larvae. The size of the individual cells will vary depending upon the bees and their needs. We will talk a bit more about that later.

Who is in charge? A hive of bees seems to function as a single individual yet contains upwards of 60,000 bees. Some wild hives will even reach mammoth proportions of double or triple that depending on the location and how comfortable they feel with their surroundings. If there is space, safety, food and water, the colony can grow fairly large. An average beehive kept by a beekeeper will have between 50,000 and 80,000 bees. All the bees in the colony take their cues from the queen. A strong colony with a healthy queen is called a queenright colony.

How do all this little creatures know what to do and when to do it? That question is one of the great mysteries of nature. Although scientists aren't exactly sure how all the bees are able to work together to create and maintain their home, they do know that most of the cues are given by the queen. The queen bee produces several different pheromones which direct the worker bees as to what activities need to be done. The pheromones tell the workers to build wax, care for brood, forage and store supplies. They also alert the workers that the queen is ailing and might need to be replaced.

The queen is not the only one giving off clues. The worker

bees also produce pheromones that create just the situation most people have the greatest fear of—a bee attack. The brood (bee larvae and pupae) even give off pheromones that tell the workers how old they are and what they need for food. It seems that pheromones help the bees manage each other, but most scientists and beekeepers agree that the queen bee is the most important bee in the hive. Although she can be usurped at any time if the colony decides she is weak or ailing, without a queen, the colony will dwindle and die off.

The honeybee definitely communicates within the hive. As we have already seen, pheromones are one major form of communication between the various bees. The pheromones give clues to the surrounding bees as to what needs to be done and how urgently it needs to get done. But it seems the honey bee also communicates through dance. When foraging worker bees return to the hive, they dance on the honeycomb. The style of dance tells the other bees how far away the food is and in what direction it lies. It appears that the frequency of repetition as well as the direction of the dance gives clues to the surrounding sisters that allow them to find the same food sources. As they dance, the bees take slight pauses to give their sisters a taste of the food source. Just like at a big box store on a weekend day where they are handing out food samples to tempt you into buying their delicious food, if the worker bees enjoy their sample enough, they may just take a flight out to collect more of the same.

The bee body is a classic insect structure consisting of a head, a thorax, and an abdomen. In a bit more detail we find the following things on a bee's body.

The head is the smallest of the three parts. On the head are two compound eyes, two antennae, and two mandibles which are sometimes referred to as mouthparts.

The thorax of the bee is the next smallest body section. Attached to it are the wings and the legs. Each wing consists of a front and back wing which are attached to each other on their respective sides. The front and back wings beat in tandem. The forelegs come out from the front of the thorax, and are articulated— which means they are jointed. They are used to clean the bee's eyes as well as the antennae. The middle legs sit in the middle of the thorax and are also articulated. They clean the thorax and the wings. The hind legs are the most specialized of the leg sets. These legs have amazing pollen baskets which collect the pollen and bring it back to the hive. If you watch your honey bees as they land in your hive, you can see the pollen baskets stuffed full of bright pollens. I love to watch for all the different colors of pollens as they come in for a landing. The pollen baskets are actually hollows in the hind leg that are surrounded by long curved hairs.

The abdomen of the bee is the largest part of the bee body and contains all the vital organs. It also carries the sting. This retractable stinger is used to inject venom from the venom sac into poor, unsuspecting victims. Just kidding—the honey bee is actually very mild and will only sting when backed into a figurative corner. In my time as a beekeeper, wearing the correct clothing, I rarely get stung. In the past three years I have only been stung once.

Three Makes One

Who runs the hive? How does the hive operate? Who does all the work? These are questions that need to be answered so you know what is going on in your hive and how the command structure within your hive is organized.

The Queen

The queen is the center of the universe for the colony. Without her, the colony becomes listless, weak and eventually dies off. With her, all the activities of the worker bees have greater urgency; the colony thrives and produces honey, wax, pollen and propolis in abundance. The queen bee is literally the mother of the entire colony.

A queen's life starts out as just another egg. Based on subtle clues, the worker bees decide the time is ripe for an insurrection. They build a queen cup, which is a hex that is slightly larger than the average comb hex and hangs vertically from the honeycomb instead of horizontally like the normal hex cell. The reigning queen comes along and lays an egg in this special hex cell. The egg is nothing special; if treated and fed like all the other eggs, it would merely become another worker bee. But, the workers want something special for this egg. If conditions are right, this egg will become queen in less than thirty days. After the egg is deposited in the cup, it will sit there for three days. Just like any other egg, after three days the egg will hatch into a larva. The workers begin to feed this special future royalty exclusively with royal jelly. Every other larva gets a bit of royal jelly in their diet, but the future queen eats only royal jelly. On the ninth day after being laid, the workers come and cap the wax hex. On the sixteenth day, the new virgin queen is ready to emerge from her cell. She chews off the top of her cell and comes forth in all her regal splendor.

Immediately, she has a fight on her hands…er, legs. She will seek out the current queen and begin a fight to the death. The loser dies. The winner rules. Often, when the worker bees sense a change in the air, they will produce six to twelve of these future queens. Mother Nature seems to feel a bit of back up is in order in case the first virgin queen to emerge loses the battle with the old monarch.

The first virgin queen to emerge and then win the battle against the reigning royal will seek out any unemerged queen larvae and sting them to death in their cells. This ensures that she rules supreme, for in the bee hive there can only be one queen.

The virgin queen takes her maiden flight within a few days. She will choose a calm, sunny day. Up she flies to a nearby "drone congregation area". There she will mate in flight with between twelve and twenty drones. She is able to store upwards of 6 million sperm in her spermatheca and will use these over the next years of her life to fertilize her amazing egg laying habit. After mating, which she only does this once, she returns to the hive and within three days begins to lay up to an astounding 2000 eggs every day during the spring build up. This number can fluctuate a bit, but over her lifetime, a healthy queen will lay millions of eggs. She can control the sex of the eggs and will carefully lay just a few drones for every thousand worker bees. The queen spends the rest of her life laying eggs. She does nothing else. Her every need is attended to by the worker bees that surround her for the rest of her life. They feed her, carry off her waste and distribute her queen mandibular pheromone—which is the pheromone that lets the hive all know the queen is on the throne and she is doing well.

INTERESTING NOTE: A virgin queen will often pipe. This is a vibrational signal similar to quacking or tooting. Right before she emerges, a virgin queen will make a G# sound in a two second pulse followed by a series of 1/4 second toots. For some reason, before a virgin queen emerges from her cell the signal is more like a quacking. Once emerged, the sound becomes more like a toot. Both sounds are referred to as piping. Piping is thought to be a battle cry calling forth any competitors to battle. Interestingly enough, a mated queen that is introduced into a new hive also will pipe. Most experts think it is the way she signals to the workers in the hive that she is a valid ruler.

The Drone

The honey bee drone is the male bee. The drone takes the longest to fully develop. After being laid as an egg, it turns to a larva in three days. On the 11th day the larva is capped and doesn't emerge until the 24th day. The drone is larger than the worker bee and is most recognizable by its large eyes. The drone's eyes are twice as large as the eyes of the worker bee. Curiously enough, the drone doesn't have a stinger. The drone has only one job in the hive, to fertilize queens. Because they have relatively little utility to the hive, in most hives there will only be somewhere between 300 and 700 drones. Almost never will you find more than 1000 drones in one hive. If you find more, it may be indicative of a missing queen and a laying worker bee or it could be the rare occurrence of a queen bee that is unable to fertilize her eggs even though she has mated. We'll discuss these problems later in the book in the chapter titled Spring—Busy as a Bee.

The drones will not typically mate with a virgin queen from

their own hive, instead they seem to "hang out" in drone congregation areas and wait for a virgin queen to arrive. Think Main Street on a Saturday night in any small town. Boys waiting for girls, what seems to be a recurring theme in nature. No one really understands how these congregation areas get chosen, but they are where the drone's life purpose is accomplished. Mating occurs midflight, about 200 to 300 feet in the air. Here is where his big eyes come in handy. The first drone to see a passing virgin queen is normally the first to achieve their life ambition. When a virgin queen passes by on her nuptial flight, the drones make their move. A drone will mate with the queen in a period of about 5 seconds and then he dies. Sadly, his man part is torn away in the ecstasy of the moment and he subsequently falls to his death.

The vast majority of the drones in a hive never accomplish their main life goal of mating with a queen. Instead, in the parsimonious manner so often found in nature, the hive refuses to share precious resources with the useless drone through the winter and instead, evict them from the hive in the fall. No drones live through this mass eviction—and the hive is drone-less until early next spring when the queen begins to lay drone eggs again.

If you watch your hive carefully in the fall, you will see two, three or even more of the worker bees wrestle the drones out of the hive. One by one, the drones are pulled and pushed from the hive. Once outside, the worker bees take flight, dragging the hapless drone to his doom. Some distance away from the hive, the workers abandon the drone and fly back to the safety of the hive. The drone is unable to find his way home and becomes food for passing birds or succumbs to the harsh environment.

The Worker

The mighty worker bee may be the smallest in size but does the lion's share of the work in the colony. Most of the colony will consist of worker bees. If there are 50,000 bees in one colony, there will be one queen, maybe 500 drones and the rest will be worker bees.

The industrious little worker bee starts her life off as an egg in a honeycomb cell, just like the queen and the drones. At three days, she becomes a larva and at 9 days her cell gets capped. On the 21st day, she emerges and her life of work begins immediately. The first chore is to get her brood cell clean. I sometimes wonder if one of her sisters walks by and says, "Mom said to make your bed and clean your room." Whatever mechanism clues her in, it seems to work well. She spends the first day or two cleaning her cell and others around the area. The queen will not lay another egg into a brood cell that isn't perfectly spotless. So if it doesn't get done right, the workers must clean it again until it passes inspection.

Days 3 through 11, in the worker bee's life, are spent feeding bee larvae. The nurse bee, as it is referred to during this stage, feeds worker jelly to worker larvae. During this same period of time, if there are any drones or queen bee larvae that need to be fed, they will receive royal jelly. Queen larva get only royal jelly, drones get the good stuff for just three days. The workers produce this royal jelly and the worker jelly with the same glands.

On the 12th day, the humble, busy little worker bee begins to produce wax. It will spend until day 17 building new honeycomb, repairing old honeycomb and capping stored honey and pollen as well as capping larva that are ready for that event. The wax is produced from four sets of wax glands that are found in her abdomen. If you look carefully in your hive, you will see some of the bees have flakes of wax on their bodies. This is normal. As the wax is produced, it forms in small flakes on the worker bee's body.

The next few days, up until day 22, are spent defending the hive. The guard bees stand in the entrance of the hive and check the scent of every entrant. Any who try to enter without the hive smell will be attacked. This can include bees from other hives, flies, hornets, wasps, and even you if you don't enter the hive properly.

We'll discuss opening the hive a little later. For now, be reassured that if done properly, the defenders of the hive will not be able to do you harm.

Other activities that the worker bees will engage in during their lives are:

1. Feeding drones (the lazy guys can't even feed themselves at first and don't start feeding themselves until older),

2. Care for the queen by feeding her, cleaning her, and collecting the critical Queen Mandibular Pheromone that seems to manage the hive.

3. Seal mature honey in cells. This wax cell, or cap, prevents the honey from absorbing moisture from the air. Because honey is hygroscopic, it will absorb moisture from the air. High moisture content will ferment and spoil the honey. To prevent this, the bees seal the honey with a bit of wax called a cap once the honey gets to the perfect moisture content.

4. Collect wax to build and repair honeycomb.

5. Pack collected pollen firmly into honeycomb and mix it with just a touch of honey. The honey keeps it from spoiling.

6. Act as morticians by removing dead bees and larvae from

the hive. This obsession with cleanliness keeps the hive safe from diseases.

7. Fan the hive to keep it cool and to help the honey reach the perfect state of moisture content.

8. Propolize the hive. Propolis is a resinous substance that the bees collect from plants and mix with enzymes from the bees. Propolis has antibacterial as well as antifungal properties. They basically use it to glue up any cracks and crevices in the hive walls.

9. Carry water to the hive. They spread this water onto the backs of the bees that are fanning. The fanning bees become miniature evaporative coolers; this helps the hive stay cool.

On the 22nd day, the worker bee graduates into a foraging or field bee. As a forager, these bees are responsible for finding and bringing nectar, pollen, water and resin for propolis into the hive. Amazingly, bees can travel up to 1.5 miles to find these important items. Of course, if they can find it closer, they will. Her life ends when her wings are literally worked ragged and she becomes unable to fly anymore. When this happens, she usually is unable to return to the hive and perishes soon after. A sad end for our noble little worker.

*While this timeline for the worker bee is accurate, depending on the needs of the hive the individual workers may spend more or less time doing certain activities.

The worker bee has a busy life. Every single moment of it is spent working for the good of the hive. Let's talk for a moment about her role as defender of the hive.

The worker bee has a stinger with a barb. When she stings a mammal, the barb catches under the skin and stays in place. As she pulls away, her abdomen tears open and the venom bulb stays hanging from the barb. During this event, an alarm pheromone is released by the Koshevnikov gland. This alarm alerts nearby sisters to come and join the defensive effort. The pheromone will encourage other bees to sting. The venom bulb attached to the stinger continues to pulse and push more venom into the victim until it is empty or removed. The bee, broken and torn, dies from her effort to defend her sisters. The barb is constructed in such a way that when a bee uses it on other insects, it doesn't get stuck. So invading insects beware, you will be stung many times and no bees will be harmed in the process.

A few interesting facts for you to consider as you think about the worker bee:

- She will visit about 1500 flowers to collect a full load of pollen. A full load weighs about 10 mg.

- The colony must produce approximately 500,000 flakes of wax to equal one pound of beeswax

- She will produce approximately 1/12 of a teaspoon of honey during her entire life.

- She flies about 15 miles per hour.

- One ounce of honey would give a single bee enough energy to fly around the world, if only she could fly that far.

- She and her sisters will visit about 2 million flowers to produce a pound of honey. So be appropriately grateful, when you get 100 pounds of honey from your hive, they have visited upwards of 200 million flowers to give you that wonderful gift of golden joy.

Bees live their lives in stages. When first laid, they spend the first three days as an egg. As an egg, they subsist on the yolk in their individual egg. From there, they hatch into a larva. During their short period of time as a larva, they stay in the honeycomb cell they were laid in and eat and are nourished by the worker bees in the hive. The first three days as a larva they are fed royal jelly. After this, the worker bees begin to receive bee jelly, honey and pollen—sometimes referred to as bee bread. During this stage of growth, amazing things are happening to her body. She grows to a size 1500 time larger than when she was first laid as an egg by the queen. During this period of time, all bee castes molt nearly every 24 hours. They will molt five times as a larva. At the appropriate time, worker bees come along and cap the cell with wax. Sealed in her wax chamber, the larva spins herself into a cocoon and becomes quiet and still. On the 20th day, she has her sixth molt and is now considered an imago (adult) bee. The next day she chews her way out of her wax cell and emerges ready to work in the hive.

Hive Produce

What is produced in a honeybee hive? There are several items that get produced by a colony of bees; including, most notably, honey.

Honey is simply a sweet food made by the bees from flower nectar. They collect the nectar and when they return home store it in the honeycomb. The nectar is then transformed into honey by a process of regurgitation and evaporation. For the bees, it is their primary food source. For us humans, it is a delicious food source that is approximately the same sweetness as granulated sugar. Many people use it as a sugar substitute when baking.

The flavor of the honey is highly affected by the source of the nectar. Different trees and flowers produce different flavors of honey. For most hobbyist and even professional beekeepers, their honey will be classified as wildflower honey. The wildflower honey designation means that multiple types of flowers were visited by the bees to collect their nectar. If the bees are in an area where they visit only one type of flower or tree, that honey can be classified as such. For instance, a hive in the middle of an apricot orchard several acres large could possibly be labeled as apricot honey. Some of these specialty honeys are absolutely sublime.

Honey is often used as a sugar substitute. Self-sufficiency is one of the reasons I first started keeping bees. Most estimates for food requirements state around 50-60 pounds of sugar is sufficient for one person for a year. Using an average of 100 pounds of honey per beehive per year, a beehive or two, or even three or four might just be able to produce all the sweetener you and your family need for a year. If you get really excited about beekeeping, excess honey can be sold often for nearly $7 a pound since your honey is local and fresh. With even 10 hives you could be producing nearly $7000 worth of honey each year. Many professional beekeepers have started out just this way. Starting with just one or two hives and slowly growing their collection of hives into a full time occupation.

Bees also produce wax. This wax is used by the bees to create their beautiful homes. For humans, the wax represents a useful and profitable resource. Beeswax is used in making many cosmetics, candles and many other things. For the bees to produce a pound of wax they must consume about 24 pounds of honey. To accomplish this feat, they must fly a collective 150,000 miles to gather the food energy to make the pound of wax. So your wax is precious. Some beekeepers take as much wax as they can every year during harvest. Others prefer their honey bees to produce more honey and less wax. They try and take as little wax as possible during harvest time. The wax you collect will mostly be in the form of cappings. These are the tiny caps the bees use to seal the honey in the honeycomb. If your harvest produces about 100 pounds of honey, you may have approximately 2 pounds of wax from cappings. The more you take during harvest, the more your bees will need to produce the following year.

Pollen is collected by worker bees as they fly from flower to flower. Once the bees collect the pollen, they mix it with a bit of honey and then store it in the honeycomb for when it is needed as food for the larvae. Sometimes this pollen and honey mixture is called bee bread. Bee pollen contains all 22 of the elements that compose the human system. Because of this, it has been used as a food for thousands of years. Almost every culture has hailed bee pollen as a therapeutic remedy. It contains almost all of the B complex vitamins as well as several minerals and trace elements. Composed of 55% carbohydrates, 35% protein, 3% vitamin and minerals and 2% fatty acids, the pollen is much sought after as a health food. Some people even claim that small amounts of pollen eaten daily help inoculate them against the worst effects of seasonal allergies. It has no known side effects.

Propolis is another wonderful product we get from our bees. A resinous mixture that bees collect from plants and flowers, propolis is used to reinforce the beehive, seal alternate entrances to make the hive more defensible, and to inhibit fungal and bacterial growth within the hive. It is also used by the bees to inhibit vibrations in the hive.

Although the thought of propolis as a health substance has proponents as well as opponents, modern science has shown it to have antimicrobial properties that seem to help with a wide variety of ailments including cold sores and mouth pain. It is also widely used as an oral hygiene product that helps protect against cavities and other oral disease. It is also touted as useful in fighting stomach and intestinal disorders as well as some wounds and burns. Some studies have even shown a possible use in the fight against cancer.

Propolis is quite sticky when the temperature is above 68 degrees Fahrenheit. Below that temperature it becomes hard and brittle. You will quickly see this when you open your hive in the cooler temperatures. Sometimes, after the bees have sealed the boxes together with propolis, you will hear a loud crack when you break the propolis seal.

Get Ready, Get Set, Go

Your Apiary Plan

The most important thing when planning your new apiary is to consider the location of your hive. Although bees are hardy little creatures that seem to survive and even thrive in nearly every condition, they definitely do much better when the conditions are perfect. In my area of the world, it is very hot through the summer and extremely dry. Winters can be cold and sometimes last extra long. This weather limits hive production somewhat. For me, a harvest of over 100 pounds is pretty spectacular. I have heard that beekeepers in the Southern United States, where the bees keep working year round, can sometimes gather over 200 pounds per hive. So location does make a difference. You probably aren't going to move just to find a better climate for your bees, but even within your climate, the microclimate you place your bees in can make a dramatic difference in your harvest.

I can attest that proper hive placement can mean the difference between a paltry harvest of only ten pounds and a bumper crop of over 100 pounds. My second year keeping bees, I had two hives within eight feet of each other. One hive produced over 80 pounds of honey and the other produced just 10 pounds of honey. The extra bit of morning sun made all the difference to the higher producing hive. Choose your spot carefully; the microclimate of the perfect spot can make all the difference.

When you get ready to place your hive, look for a location that gets early morning sunshine, some shade through the hottest part of the day and a bit more sunshine as the sun sinks slowly in the west. The middle of the day is the hottest time. If the sun beats down on your beehive, they will be somewhat lethargic and less likely to keep working. Most studies agree that bees prefer an ideal temperature of 72° F. They don't even fly when the temperature is below about 50° F and they get really lazy when the temperature gets above 100° F. Actually, they sound a bit like me.

If you can place your hive where they get some direct sunlight right when the sun comes up, it will get the hive active early. Then, as the sun rises to midday, if the hive gets some tree shade it will be ideal. A bit of light late into the summer days keeps them working late.

Your bees need water to survive. They use it for a wide variety of purposes including these most important three things:

- They use it to cool the hive. Not only do they put it on the backs of the fanning bees to create mini evaporative coolers, they also place it around capped brood within the hive and then fan it to keep the larvae cool.

- The nurse bees drink it like they are kids out in the summer sun. The nurse bees eat a combination of pollen, honey and water to produce both royal jelly and bee jelly. This is used to feed the larvae.

- Finally, the bees use the water to decrystallize honey. Over time, all honey will crystallize. When this happens, the bees use water to dissolve the crystals so they can eat the honey.

During the hottest days of the summer, a beehive can use over a quart of water a day just to survive. When the forager bees bring back water, they take their clues from the bees in the hive. If the bees gather the water quickly from the foragers, the foragers realize the need is high and head back out for more. If they get left standing around for a while, they sense that less water is needed and may gather nectar and pollen the next trip out.

The bees need a local source of water. And as a side note, if your neighbor swimming pool or their hose bib is the closest source of water, that is exactly where your bees will head. Make sure your bees have a clean, fresh source of water nearby, so they don't hang around your neighbor's pool or hose bib. This can be as simple as a small bucket of water to a full bee pond. Be aware that bees don't swim so well. So put a few rocks in the water that just poke above the surface the bees will have an easier time collecting the water. They can stand safely on the rocks and collect water without the danger of drowning.

Also, although the bees like water, they don't like too much. If your bees feel the area is just too wet and clammy, it is entirely possible they will get up and leave. This isn't a huge problem, just be aware that the bees don't like wet and slimy conditions. I have had beehives right next to sprinklers for many years and have never had a problem with too much water—but I do one thing to make it right for the bees. I tilt the beehive just slightly forward. That way, if too much water does get into the hive during a thunderstorm or for some other reason, it will roll on out. If you live in a harsh winter environment, this is critical. Inside the hive, where it is warm, water condensation will form. If the condensed water drips down on the bees or collects in a corner of the hive, it will be uncomfortable and possibly deadly for your hive. Tilt the hive forward. My hives have a difference of about a half inch from front to back, with the back being a bit higher. That bit of tilt makes all the difference in the world to their well-being as it helps keep the hive dry.

If you want your bees to be extra happy, find a locale where there are plentiful sources of food. It will amaze you how many different trees, shrubs and flowers the bees will locate. Don't worry excessively about this, but if you want to plant a few extra flowers in your garden, the bees will appreciate it.

What things should you consider when placing your hive? Consider that wherever you place your hive, there will be a steady stream of bees leaving and entering the hive throughout the day. Bees, interestingly enough, when they leave the hive, will fly above any obstacles that are nearby and then stay at that level until they arrive at their destination. If you want your bees to fly above people instead of knee high, you can place your hive so there is an obstacle a few feet in front of it. If there is a six foot fence about five to ten feet in front of the hive, the bees will fly up to "clear" the obstacle and then will happily fly at that altitude until they get to the flower patch where their work awaits. For the urban beekeeper this fact is extra important. Bees flying up high will rarely even be noticed by locals. Remember the old saying, "Out of sight, out of mind."

Another thing to consider is that although you aren't allergic to bee stings, (right—we already sorted that possibility out?) you may have visitors that are allergic. A wise idea is to visit your local doctor and explain that you are planning on keeping bees. Most doctors will happily write you a prescription for an EpiPen. It makes sense to keep one on hand in case of an emergency.

What about getting stung? As a beekeeper, you are going to get stung. For the average person, a bee sting hurts and itches for a few minutes or more. A small red bump can develop. This doesn't mean you are allergic—it is the normal reaction to a bee sting. (Someone with a true allergy will begin to swell rapidly and may begin to struggle to breath. This is not normal and the person needs immediate help. Get them an EpiPen and get them immediately to the hospital.) Over time, most beekeepers actually build up a tolerance to bee stings and they bother less and less. But, if you get stung, here are some basic things to do to lessen the bother.

Don't try and pull the stinger out. You invariably squeeze it and push more venom out of the venom sac, through the stinger, and into your body. Instead, try and scrape across the skin where the stinger is with a credit card or something similarly stiff. This normally will scrape the stinger out of your skin and prevent more venom from being pumped into you.

Next apply some ice. Cold water also helps. If you are concerned, you can take some antihistamine medicine. Or, if you prefer, here are a few natural methods purported to work wonders on the spot of a bee sting.

- Apply freshly squeezed garlic juice to the sting.
- Mix baking soda and water to make a paste. Apply the paste to the skin. I have an aunt that uses a variation on this; she mixes meat tenderizer with water. I have used it and it works wonderfully.
- Apply freshly crushed plantain (Plantago) leaf to the sting. You can crush it by smashing it with your fingers or

just chew it a bit. I have used this also and it works wonderfully.

- Crushed basil leaves are supposed to reduce the pain.
- Use a cotton ball soaked in vinegar. Tape it on the spot of the sting or use a band aid to fasten it. Leave it for about 30 minutes.

No matter what precautions you take as a beekeeper, you are going to get stung from time to time. The best way to deal with the anxiety that you may feel about stings is to take the appropriate steps to reduce the likelihood of getting stung while you work with your bees. Here are some basic things to do.

First, always wear your gear. The first time I thought I would just get into my hive real quick and look at it without the gear was the last time I chose to work on my hives without gear. It was an unmitigated disaster. I think my wife still laughs about the sight of me running full bore around the corner of the house and dashing into the house. I removed plenty of bee stings that morning. Wear your gear—you will feel more calm and protected and the bees will feel your calm.

Second, use your smoker. We will get into why it helps later, but it definitely helps keep the colony on a calm footing.

Third, work on a clear, warm day when possible. If it is too cold or hot outside, your bees will be a bit grumpier when you get into the hive. Think how you would like someone to lift the roof off your house in the middle of the winter or summer. Not fun for them equals not fun for you.

Fourth, wear light colored clothes. Bees seem to associate dark colors with predators. If you can wear a light colored shirt that is best.

Fifth, move slow and easy. For the same reason as the colors, bees seem to associate fast movement with predators and will attack if you are moving fast. Take it slow and easy and things will be just fine.

Sixth, realize that no matter what happens, the bees are going to sting your clothes. This doesn't mean you are getting stung, just your clothes. Don't panic when this happens, just keep working.

Finally, no matter what you do, one day you are going to be working and you will realize a bee is in your veil. Don't panic, she probably feels as concerned as you do. Just keep moving slow and easy. If you need to move away from the hives, do so. Then take your veil off and brush her gently away. Then get back in there and get the work done.

Time for a bee sting story. I was pretty new at keeping bees. It was only my second year and my father in law wanted to get a hive. So I went over to help him get set up. A couple months later, he was ready for a honey harvest. I went over to supervise and help if the need arose. I was giving him a bit of a hard time because he had a full body suit. It wasn't your normal bee suit. He was wearing a tyvek painter suit. The ambient temperature that day was about 95° F and inside his suit he had to be around 120°. I was giving him grief about it. He just smiled and kept working. A few minutes later, we were moving one of his boxes and a bee landed on my pants. Unaware that disaster loomed on the horizon, I continued to tease my father in law about his suit. The bee that had landed on my pants started her attack. She crawled up my pants leg and promptly stung me on the one area where no man wants to be stung. As I cried out in pain, I wondered if I should strike the offending bee. Quickly deciding that would only compound the problem, I wondered if the neighbors would think it strange if I pulled my pants down in the middle of my father in laws yard. Deciding that wasn't in anyone's best interest, I chose to grin and bear it. In the end, I just suffered quietly. My manhood stung and my humiliation was complete, but I learned two valuable lessons. First, a rubber band around your pant leg will keep bees from climbing up and stinging you in that oh so tender location. And two, don't ever tease your father in law about his Tyvek suit—it is hot but it keeps the stingers away from the jewels. The law of comeuppance is swift and sometimes painful.

We will go into a whole lot more detail about pests in the chapter on Diseases, Pests and Other Problems. But right now, you should consider if you have any issues with local wildlife. From my experience, most domestic animals will quickly learn not to pester the bees. I even keep chickens in the same space as some of my hives and they have learned to coexist rather well. But you should be aware that some animals just like to eat honey. Ants, mice, raccoons, skunks, some birds and even bears can all cause problems with your hives. When you are placing your hive, there are certain things you can do to ameliorate the issues you may potentially have with marauders. If you think your area may have issues with any of the aforementioned pests, skip over to the section on pests right now and read up on the possible animal problems and what you can do to prevent issues. If you live in the middle of the city, you probably won't have any issues and can read about pests later. For now, let's get on to the exciting second chapter Get Ready, Get Set, Go, and learn all about what gear we need to get started and how to get our very first hive all set up for bees.

Gearing Up

You have a choice. You can either build your hive or you can purchase it already assembled. As somewhat of a handyman, and as someone who has done it both ways, I suggest the first time around, you purchase your hive already assembled. The assembly isn't particularly difficult, but I found that the time invested far outweighed the difference in price between pre-assembled boxes and frames versus unassembled. But, to each their own. If you want to put yours together, it isn't hard, and you will save a bit of money. Plus it is a good time to spend with significant others or children talking about the upcoming adventure. I found that my children enjoyed helping me glue and nail the parts together when I purchased unassembled parts. Because they had the chance to help, they felt more a part of the process and I think it made the honey sweeter for everyone involved.

If you get really ambitious, you can actually find plans online to build your own from scratch. This involves lots of sawing and cutting. I think it would be advantageous to go this route if you were going to have several hundred hives—the savings would be significant. But otherwise, I would steer clear so that a much anticipated project doesn't turn into a dreaded chore that drags on for weeks. On the other end of the spectrum, you can buy basic startup kits that have everything you need to get started, all assembled and ready to go right into your yard. These kits will typically have a bit of a premium in cost, but may be worth it if you just want to dive in with the least amount of fuss and bother.

There are several basic parts to each hive. Let's go through those in order, working from the bottom up to the top.

1. Hive Stand

2. Bottom Board

3. Slatted Rack (Optional)

4. Lower Brood Chamber

5. Upper Food Chamber

6. Frames and wax foundation for both these Chambers

7. Queen Excluder (Somewhat Optional)

8. Honey Super #1

9. Honey Super #2

10. Frames and wax foundation for both these supers

11. Inner Cover

12.   Outer Cover

Let's go through each part so you have a clear picture of what the purpose of the part is.

The Hive Stand is the base of the hive. It is quite simply a four sided open box with the front piece of the box at a slant. The slanted part provides a convenient landing spot for incoming bees. In the heat of the summer, the bees will spill out onto this entryway and cool off.

The Bottom Board is a board that sits on top of the hive stand. Essentially a board with three side walls attached, it creates a space between the lower brood chamber and the hive stand so the bees can enter the hive.

A slatted rack creates extra air space for the hive. It measures about an inch thick and sits between the bottom board and the lower brood chamber. Some people swear they help the queen lay more efficiently. I never have used them and seem to do just fine without. If you start without them and find your queen needs a bit of help, it is easy enough to add one later. Your call on using this part or not.

The Lower Brood Chamber and the Upper Brood Chamber

are hive boxes. All hive boxes can also be referred to as supers. Some beekeepers will only refer to hive boxes that are specifically intended for honey as supers and others will call all the hive boxes supers. In reality, there are three standard size hive boxes. Deep, Medium, and Shallow. The deep boxes are 19 7/8" by 16 3/4". A deep box is 9 5/8" deep and can weigh up to 80 pounds when full. A medium box is 6 6/8" deep and weighs about 50 pounds when full. A shallow box is 5 11/16" deep and weighs about 40 pounds when full. Many commercial beekeepers get all deep boxes. It makes the two hive boxes and the two super boxes interchangeable—which with a big operation makes things easier. Both the lower brood chamber and the upper food chamber should be the deep size boxes. Inside each, you will have either nine or ten frames. Each frame contains a layer of wax foundation to help the bees get started and "train" them to build honeycomb in the right places. The frames hang inside the box and provide the bees with preset walls on which to build their honeycomb.

If you want to make things really easy, just get four deep boxes. The issue becomes the honey supers. A deep box being used as a honey super can weigh over 80 pounds when full. So if that is going to be too heavy for you to move during harvest time, then consider getting medium or even shallow boxes for your supers. You can put on as many supers as you want, so instead of two deep supers you could use four shallow. I even mix and match my medium and deep on my hives, but I always use two deep for my hive body and you should as well. That way, your bees have all the room they need to set up shop and keep the queen happy.

On top of the Food Chamber or second main body box you can put a queen excluder. This is a somewhat controversial piece to your hive. Some people swear by them, others just swear at them. The queen excluder is simply a wire or wood frame with a wire grid inside the frame that is spaced close enough to allow worker bees through but too close to allow the queen through. What this means is that the queen can't get up into the super boxes. The argument for is that it prevents you from dealing with brood in your honey harvest. Since the queen can't get up into the super boxes, she can't lay any eggs up there. The argument against is the old saying that the queen won't cross honey to lay. Remember the shape of the hive? Essentially a basketball sized ball of larvae and brood comb surrounded by a thin layer of pollen which is then surrounded by a large layer of honey. The queen generally won't cross that layer of honey to go lay eggs higher up in the hive. The other part of the argument against is that a queen excluder bothers the worker bees and they don't like to cross it. So the opponents of queen excluders claim you get less honey. I use the queen excluder and except for one time have never had a problem. I got very lazy one year with one of my hives and didn't check it in June. By the time I checked it in late July, I realized the bees had built comb in a strange horizontal configuration blocking access to the super boxes. No access for the bees to the upper supers meant no honey in them. I don't know if the queen excluder caused this problem or not, but it wouldn't have been a problem if I had just checked my hive in June like I usually do.

On top of the queen excluder go the two or three or even four or five super boxes. I usually just use two large supers but sometimes I use three medium supers. I ended up with a variety of different sized boxes over the years and just use them as I need them. But, remember, a full large box weighs 70+ pounds. That is a whole lot to lift, especially when in a bee suit and sometimes lifting at strange angles. It's up to you—but remember what your mother used to tell you— "better safe than sorry". If you aren't sure about lifting the weight, just get medium or small boxes for your honey supers.

On top of the highest super goes an inner cover. This is a four sided frame with a solid horizontal board that acts as a top to the hive. The inner cover has an oval hole so the bees can leave the hive. From there, the crawl across the board and exit the hive out a small slot in the edge of the frame. This hole acts as a ventilation hole as well as a secondary exit to the hive.

On top of the inner cover goes the outer cover. These come in a wide variety of styles and designs. Basically it is a top with four small slats that is just a bit bigger than the inner cover so it sits down on top of the hive and keeps the weather out. Most have galvanized steel on top so they last a long time. I even have one with copper. It was my first hive and I thought it looked really neat. It does, and I love it. But the cost of the copper is a bit more and my subsequent hives just have flat galvanized covers that are more utilitarian and definitely easier on the budget.

Now come the other hive pieces that are used only occasionally. There are, in no particular order:

1. Hive reducer

2. Feeder (Top, entrance, or frame)

3. Hive Stand, Elevated

I have all these parts and use none of them. But, you may or may not need them. It depends on your area and your particular hives. The hive reducer is simply a board that covers most of the main entrance to the hive. When the colony is brand new, it prevents aggressive pests like wasps or other hives from attacking and destroying your colony. I have never needed one, but if I ever did really anything would work. I have even heard of some people just grabbing a bunch of grass and knotting it up and stuffing it in the entrance to cover most of the hole. By reducing the size of the hole, you allow the bees a smaller hole to defend. Get one if you are worried, but if you don't get one, don't worry about it.

The various feeders allow you to get your colony off to a running start. I do recommend a feeder. I prefer the entrance feeder because it is the least invasive. To refill it, I don't have to open up the hive. The top feeder is the next least invasive and the frame feeder is the most. I have used all three, and now I just do it the lazy man's way. When my bees need extra food, I fill a two gallon bucket with sugar water and stick it close to the hive. I throw a few packing peanuts into the sugar water so the bees can land on them and drink the sugar water without drowning. This seems to be the easiest way for me to feed my bees. The buckets are cheap and they work just fine. Some people worry that it will attract other bees to the area. I have never had an issue. In fact, I often just use one bucket for a bunch of hives when they are relatively close together. All the hives seem to leave each other alone. They just fly in, get their sugar water, and head out. But, once again, if you want a feeder, by all means get one. I would go with the entrance feeder. It is the simplest to use and refill. If you live in a really cold area, you may at some time need a feeder that fits inside the hive. In this case I would suggest a top feeder so you don't let in too much cold if you feed your bees during the winter.

Finally an elevated hive stand. This is a convenience. Quite simply, by raising the hive up you put it closer to you so you don't have to bend over as much when working with your hive. It can also help defend the hive from some pests and predators. This can be a fancy set of legs or just a few bricks. Whatever works for you. I don't use hive stands but I do place my hives on a 2.0' by 1.5' piece of plywood. When the plywood finally gives up the ghost, I just throw a new piece under the hive.

So that is the full list of everything you could possibly need as far as the hive pieces. Next up is equipment for you, the beekeeper.

In an effort to keep well protected from stray stings, there are several pieces of equipment that will serve you well. The first is the bee veil. You can go very light here and just purchase the veil with an included hat. This is essentially a white hard hat with a net that hangs over it and gathers at the bottom, around your neck. This is the least expensive option. It is also the option that offers the least amount of protection, aside from no protection at all. With one of these, from time to time, a stray bee will find their way inside the veil. For the most part, once inside, they will leave you alone. But it can be a bit disconcerting while working on your hive to have a bee buzzing a couple inches or less from your face. I used one of these bee veils for a year or two but finally stepped up to a bee jacket. I feel much more comfortable with my jacket than I ever did with just the veil.

The next step up from the bee veil is a bee jacket with

included face protection. This is a relatively thick white jacket that zips up the front and has an integral hood that pulls down over your head. The hood piece zips up around your neck and prevents bees from getting in. These generally have elastic bands to keep them tight around your waist and long sleeves that Velcro strap tight onto your wrists. Worn properly, these offer all the protection you need. But they can cost nearly $100 depending on your source.

The ultimate in protection is the full body suit. This is a white jumpsuit of the same material as the jacket and also comes with an integral, full hood. The hood pieces, if you can't picture them, look a lot like the hoods that fencers wear. These full body suits cost even more, but do offer the ultimate in protection.

And there are many variations in between. As I mentioned before, my father in law wears a Tyvek painting suit with a bee veil. It gives him all the protection he needs. I used to wear just a bee veil and a long sleeve sweatshirt along with jeans. After a few too many stings, I have graduated to the bee jacket. I feel it gives me all the protection I need.

As for your hands, many people purchase long leather gloves. I have a pair of these but find them difficult to manipulate things well with my hands. I got so frustrated with my pair of specialized bee gloves that I switched over to a tight fitting pair of leather work gloves. These give my hands the protection they need just fine. I get mine at a local hardware store for just a few dollars

As for your lower body, jeans work well. Just make sure you have no holes in the jeans, because if you do, the bees will find a way in. As far as the bottom of your pant legs, there are various approaches to keep the bees from crawling up. Some people rubber band their pant legs. I used to do this all the time. Now I just pull my tube socks up over my pant legs. It looks silly but it keeps the bees from crawling up my legs. A couple of stings on your legs will convince you that it doesn't matter what you look like—as long as it keeps the bees out.

For shoes, I just wear my regular tennis shoes. Many people I know put on a good pair of leather work boots. That works fine too. Boots give you a bit more protection.

The most important part about being fully protected is that when you know the bees can't get after you and sting you, you are much calmer working on the hive. This calm flows into the hive and they react accordingly. When you feel rushed or nervous, the bees pick up on your feelings and start to really attack with some vigor.

I think I mentioned earlier about the one time I decided I could work my hive with no protection. I have a book with a picture of a beekeeper standing calmly with his hive open and looking at the bees. He is wearing just a short sleeve shirt and pants with no face or hand protection at all. I'm not sure how he managed that picture, but it isn't something I recommend.

The problem lies in the pheromones. When a bee stings something, a pheromone is released that signals to the other bees that the hive is under attack. Several more bees will now come to the area of attack and begin to get a bit aggressive. That is the whole point of the smoker. It covers the scent of the pheromone, and does something else that we will talk about here in a moment. But, when you are tempted to work on your hive without your protective gear— resist the temptation. Just put your gear on, you will be grateful you did.

What tools do you need to work on the hive? One of the most critical tools is your smoker. In fact, if you have your smoker and your protective gear, that is all you absolutely need.

The smoker is a small chamber with a spout at the top. On

the back, a bellows is attached. They come in a wide variety of sizes and styles. Essentially, what you are looking for in your smoker is durability and ease of use. Some smokers have several plastic and rubber parts. Avoid these, they won't last more than a few seasons. The very best smokers will be all metal construction and the bellows will be a nice wood or metal and material combination. The top of the smoker comes off so you can place your smoke tinder inside.

Any kind of tinder can be used, but I generally use old pieces of burlap bag or some raw cotton. Throw your tinder in, light it and place the lid back on. After a few moments, gently pump the bellows. If done properly, a light tendril of smoke will come out of the spout. You may want to practice the art of the smoker for a while before you actually get into working with your hive. It takes a bit of practice and patience. But with time and practice, you will soon become an expert at managing the level of smoke coming from your smoker. Blow too much smoke into your hive, and the bees get too restless. They may think the hive is on fire and begin to evacuate. Not en masse, but more than you really want. Too little smoke and your bees will be a bit on the aggressive side. Since I always work with my hives in full protection, I generally error on the side of too little smoke rather than too much.

The smoke does two things. First, when the bees do sting your clothing, the smoke will mask the alert pheromone released by the Koshevnikov gland. This will prevent the hive from going to full intruder alert. Second, because the bees may think the hive is threatened with fire, they begin to gorge on honey. It's their way of moving the honey in case they really do need to leave. When gorged, the little bees are on the chubby side. Just like you or I feel after a Thanksgiving supper. Because of this, their abdomens are distended and they have a difficult time doing the "crunch" necessary to sting you. You see, when bees sting, they pull their abdomen up under them and push the stinger straight down. Engorged, they are less able to accomplish this feat and you less likely to get stung. It's kind of like asking you to do some crunches right after the Thanksgiving feast. Not happening in my world and apparently not in their world either.

Whatever the reasons, the smoker will be your best friend. You can feed it wood chips, raw cotton, wet burlap, even dry grass. Just don't put anything in it that will put out a toxic smoke. That isn't nice for your bees.

The next tool you need is called a hive tool. Basically a wide, flat mini crowbar the hive tool helps you pull sticky frames out from inside the hive as well as pry boxes apart that have been glued up with loads of propolis. Sounds funny, but it is amazing how strong dried propolis is. You will actually hear a loud crack when pulling apart boxes glued up with propolis. I definitely recommend having one of these on hand whenever you get in your hive. A long, thick bladed knife will work as well, but the hive tool is perfect.

A bee brush is one of those optional tools for a regular hive check. You will need one for harvest time. It is a soft, long bristled brush that lets you sweep the bees off the hive frames. I find the bristles to be too soft for my liking. Instead, I went to the local hardware store and picked up a small hand broom—the kind you use for sweeping up sawdust in the garage. It works perfect for my needs. I only use the brush during harvest time. The rest of year, I leave it in storage.

The final necessary piece of equipment is a hive frame hanger. Essentially two clips that hang over the edge of your bee box and two other arms that extend outwards from the hive. When you have the hive open, it gives you somewhere to set frames that have already been inspected, but aren't ready to be placed back in the hive. They are extremely handy. I highly recommend having and using a hive hanger when doing hive inspections.

So here is the all inclusive list of everything you need to get started. I have broken it into two categories: Must Have Gear and Might be Nice to Have Gear. The full list is going to set you back between $200 and $600 depending on the route you take. If you are careful, only get the absolutely necessary things and even look for used equipment, you can most likely swing in at the low end of this cost structure. If you just want to get everything new and high quality, then you are probably looking at spending much closer to the high end. So here is the list.

MUST HAVE GEAR

1. Hive Stand

2. Bottom Board

3. Slatted Rack (Optional)

4. Lower Brood Chamber

5. Upper Food Chamber

6. Frames and wax foundation for both these Chambers

7. Queen Excluder (Somewhat Optional)

8. Honey Super #1

9. Honey Super #2

10. Frames and wax foundation for both these supers

11. Inner Cover

12. Outer Cover

13. Bee Veil or Bee Jacket with Veil or Bee Suit with
Veil

14. Gloves

15. Shoes or Boots

16. Smoker — Good Quality

17. Hive Tool

MIGHT BE NICE TO HAVE GEAR

1. Hive Feeder (Top, entrance, or frame)

2. Hive Reducer

3. Bee Brush

4. Hive Hanger Tool

5. Hive Stand, Elevated

6. Extractor

7. Uncapping Knife

8. Double Stainless Steel Honey Strainer

9. Uncapping Tank

10. Uncapping Fork

11. 5 Gallon honey bucket with gate valve

12. Mason Jars, honey jars or somewhere else to place

harvest

Your Bees

The only other cost you should incur is the actual bees. When you get ready to order your bees, consider the different strains of bees that are available and find the strain that most likely fits your needs. Although there are many other strains of bees aside from the ones I cover, these are the most common and I would suggest starting with one of these four—at least with your first hive.

Italian Bee

The *Apis mellifera lingustica* is the Italian Bee. A subspecies of the western honey bee (*Apis mellifera*) the Italian bee is best known for its easygoing personality and amazingly robust output. A yellow brown color with very distinct body bands, they are thought to have originated somewhere south of the Alps in Italy, hence the name. Some hives have been known to produce over 300 pounds in a single year. But it isn't all a bed of roses with the Italian bee.

Their drawbacks are that they don't form as tight of a winter ball as some other hives, which means they expend more energy to stay warm. This also means they consume more through the winter.

Additionally, they overwinter with a larger number of bees in the hive, which also contributes to their winter food needs. And, in the spring and summer, if they feel the least bit constrained by their hive, they are fairly quick to swarm.

Still, for their drawbacks, they are my favorite type of bee. If you live in a moderately warm climate and are willing to give them extra super boxes, the Italian might be the perfect choice for you. I especially like their mellow attitude.

Caucasian Bee

The Caucasian honey bee is the *Apis mellifera caucasia*. Thought to have originated in the central Caucasus, they are very common in countries such as Turkey, Armenia and Georgia. A dark lead grey in color with somewhat sporadic brown spots, these bees are considered the most mellow of the main honeybee strains. They are ideal for novice beekeepers because of their temperament. They raise strong colonies but the growth of the colony is slower than some species. This works if more of your nectar flow is in the mid to late summer, but if you have an early nectar flow in your area you should go with a different strain of bee.

They do have a few drawbacks. They use a very high amount of propolis and will really stick everything together. Also, they seem to catch the bee disease nosema more frequently than many species. And they rob like crazy. No big deal if you just have one hive, but if you are definitely going to have two or more hives, your bee area can become a little crazy as the little Caucasians sneak into other hives and attempt to steal their honey.

Carnolian Bee

The Carniolan honey bee, or *Apis mellifera carnica* comes from Slovenia, southern Austria, Hungary, Romania and Bulgaria. These bees are similar in size to the Italian but have a dusky brown grey color with light brown stripes. These bees are gentle and deal well with people. They overwinter with smaller numbers than do the Italian and so conserve their honey stores a bit better. This makes them ideal for areas with long, cold winters. They do get started early in the spring, which is good if there is a strong spring flow. For some reason, the Carniolan workers also live longer than other species.

Drawbacks are they do swarm more than other bee species if overcrowded and they don't deal well with high levels of heat. These are a great bee for a keeper that has time and patience to work with their idiosyncrasies. They are not ideal for keepers that want to have many hives or for beekeepers in hot areas.

European Brown Bee

The European Brown Bee, or *Apis mellifera mellifera,* is a big, dark colored honey bee that originated in eastern central Europe. A bigger bee than the others already discussed, the Brown Bee is more susceptible to disease. It also reacts quickly to hive intrusions. It used to be the go to bee strain among beekeepers in the Old World, but now is more of a novelty. I would steer clear of this species for your first hive.

There are many other bee species including many hybrids that seem to be popular among certain keepers. These include species such as the Buckfast, the Starline and the Midnight bees. The issue with most hybrid bees is that when the queen fails and is superseded, the new queen might not have the same genetic background. This means your hive quickly becomes something other than what you thought. And no matter what you do, at some point your queen will be overthrown. Honeybees seem to have little tolerance for long lasting monarchs.

Finally, you have the sensational Africanized bee. This is an aggressive hybrid bee that is of mixed descent from some *Apis mellifera scutellata*. These were accidentally released in 1957 down in the southeast part of Brazil. A laboratory there was trying to produce a prolific hybrid when some escaped. Overly defensive, these queens soon mated with local non-African queens and drones and have now spread throughout much of the Americas. They are actually used throughout Central America by beekeepers for honey production because they do seem to have high production levels. The bad side is they swarm more frequently, travel farther, and are more defensive and aggressive than other bee species.

They guard the hive very aggressively and send out many more guards than do other bee species. This means that if bothered, which seems to happen easily with Africanized bees, they come out swinging. Properly geared up, it shouldn't be a real problem.

Without protection, you are in for a bad time.

If you happen upon a wild hive of Africanized bees, please alert the local authorities. It appears they may be unable to survive well in colder areas, and their "advance" into the US seems to have slowed to a stop. But they are very common in many of the southern band of states.

When deciding, if you aren't absolutely sure what kind of bee you want to keep, go with the Italians. They are the most popular in the US for good reason. Calm, easy to work with, and highly productive, they do well in a wide variety of climates. The secondary benefit of keeping Italian bees is that most wild bee colonies in the US are Italian. This means that when your queen is superseded, which will happen, the new hive will probably closely resemble the old hive in temperament and productivity if you started with an Italian hive.

You can order your bees from a variety of places. It may be there is a local supplier in your area. Or, there may be someone who ships in hundreds of hives every year to sell to the local beekeepers. And of course, there is the internet. Look around a bit and do some shopping for pricing. You can expect to pay somewhere between

$50 and $70 for a packet of bees which will include the queen as well as several thousand bees. Normal shipments are three pounds of bees with a queen. Three pounds of bees amounts to about 11,000 bees.

The best time to install your bees in their new home is in early spring. Our local supplier always tells customers to call in their order on Valentine's Day. Pick up is around the third or fourth week of April. I did order once off the internet and had to place my order in October for the following spring. The packet came in the mail via USPS and I picked it up at the local post office. Getting your hive is the part that will take the most planning. Not that it is hard; you just need to know exactly when your bees will show up so that you can have everything ready for them.

My first year I purchased my bees in October, along with all my equipment. The first time around, I decided to buy everything in parts and assemble it through the winter. As things seem to go in life, I was delayed for one reason or another through the winter and remember hustling to get everything done in early April before my bees arrived. Plan carefully and hopefully you won't feel quite as rushed as I did that first time around.

As an alternative, you can also find a local beekeeper that will sell you a nucleus (nuc) colony. A standard nuc has a few frames of bees, brood, food (honey and pollen), and an active queen. The nuc will come in a box that looks just like your main hive body boxes. You just take the frames out of the nuc and put them into your hive. It takes less time, and your hive is already established so it will get up to full hive size quicker. It will be more expensive than a standard package of bees. This is a good route to go if you are starting late or just want to get an extremely strong start for your new colony.

If you are interested, there are free bees all around you. You may or may not have noticed them in your area, but I am sure they are there. There are several ways to get wild hives or swarms. The easiest way is to get on the local call list. Almost every area has a call list kept by the local or state beekeeper association. Whenever they get a call from a concerned homeowner about a swarm that has landed on their house or somewhere in their yard, they call the next interested beekeeper on the list. If your name is next, they will give you a call. Most associations don't worry too much if you can't make it when they call, they will just give the next person in line a call and put you back at the end of the list.

What do you do if you get the call? Well, put on your beekeeping equipment and head over to the address you are given. Even if you don't know much, the homeowner probably knows even less. So just act natural and get to work.

When you arrive, determine where the swarm is located. Often, they will have landed on a tree branch or bush. If this is the case, you are in a bit of luck. Other times, they land on the side of a house or outbuilding. Not as easy, but still in the realm of do able.

The swarm will most likely number between 20,000 and 40,000 or more bees. When bees swarm, a good portion of the colony's bees leave the hive with the old queen. She leaves before a new queen comes out of her cell and dethrones her. This is nature's way of growing the species.

When they leave the original hive, it is like a cyclone of bees. A great buzzing sound will start to rise to a crescendo and then thousands of bees will spill out of the hive. The swirl up and up and then fly away. The old queen is in the middle of this bee tornado. After a few hundred yards or maybe a bit more, the swarm lands. They will spend the next few hours to the next three days in this location. This is when you get the call from a panicked homeowner.

The swarm may not seem to be, but is very docile. While camping out for a few days, the swarm sends out scout bees to find the ideal new home for the swarm. As each scout returns, the hive makes a decision. Once an ideal spot is found, they all fly off and start their new home. Since there is already an old queen in place, she will begin to lay as soon as there is honeycomb available.

While they are camping out, the hive will buzz merrily and probably scare the local homeowners. But never fear, you know something they don't. The swarm isn't territorial because it has no home. And all of the bees are full up with honey, so they will have a difficult time stinging anyway. You see, before they left the old hive, they all filled up with honey so they would have enough starter food to get the new hive started.

So here is what you do. Approach the swarm gently. If you want to smoke them, that isn't a bad idea. But don't smoke them too much; you really don't want to spook the swarm. And then, if they are on a thin branch, stick a good sized cardboard box below them. Cut off the branch they are on (if that is ok with the homeowner— they are normally so worried that they would probably give you permission to raid their fridge if it would help get the bees off their property—but don't take advantage). Gently lower the branch into the box. Close the lid. Take your new swarm home and stick it in a hive box. Voila! You have a free colony of bees for a minimal amount of work.

But, if things aren't that easy, here are some more tips and tricks to help you with a swarm recovery. I have seen swarms on the ground, on a sandbox, on a tree fork and on a chain link fence to name a few locations. The toughest one was the chain link fence.

And that leads us to our funny story of the day. I left for church one Sunday a bit earlier than my family. I had a short meeting to attend before the regular church meeting. We had brand new, next door neighbors that had moved in maybe a month or less before. Between our two backyards, we have a full size vinyl fence. In the front yard, there is a chain link fence between the two yards. A huge vine grows all around and through the chain link fence; otherwise we probably would have traded it out for vinyl years ago. Anyway, my family shows up for church and tells me one of the hives has swarmed. I'm nervous out of my mind, because I have never dealt with a swarm before. And the worst news possible, in my mind at the time, was that the swarm didn't bother just leaving Dodge and heading over into the wild lands a few blocks away from our house. Instead, the old queen made it all of about 30 feet and landed with her 40,000 attendants on the chain link fence between my house and my new neighbor's house.

So when I get home from church, I look at the swarm and think, how hard can it be. I get my equipment on—this is back when I had a simple hanging bee veil instead of the full jacket. I get out to the hive, my hands are sweating and I am nervous. Nervous I'm going to really make my new neighbors mad and nervous I am about to get stung silly by this swarm.

As I get close, I realize there is no easy way to do this. The bees are all over in the individual chain links. No easy "cut-the-tree-branch-and-done" situation for me. I begin to reach in slowly and pull gobs of bees off of the fence and drop them in the box. I don't realize at the time, that if you don't have the queen in the box, the bees will just fly out of the box and get back to her. After several minutes of acting out a modern day version of Sisyphus, I realize I am making no progress and am only enraging the poor bees. There are several thousand bees now flying about in a panic. I have stirred them up into righteous indignation. And I still don't realize I need to get the queen. By now, several of the bees have stung my exposed parts. They are climbing inside my veil. I want to scream with terror. But I can't. I look into my house and there are my six beautiful children and my wonderful wife staring at me—expecting me to have success. How can I fail with them watching?

Well, after about five more minutes, which seemed like an eternity burning and stinging in the coals of Hell, I finally ran away and chickened out, seeking relief from the incessant attacks in my backyard. I licked my wounds. I read more about how to capture a swarm. And then I gave up. I meekly waited two more days for the hive to just up and leave. I was so grateful when they left. I felt like I could finally untuck my tail from between my legs and start holding my head up high again.

And from my failure, I learned a few lessons. Get a good bee jacket. You will be grateful you did. And when you work with a swarm, spend the time necessary to identify where the queen is. And then get her into your carrying box first thing. If you do, everything else will be smooth sailing. If you fail to get her, like I failed in my first bee swarm retrieval effort, then you will eventually end up angering 40,000 bees and you may pay a bit of a price for your failure.

I don't share this story with you to make you nervous. I have collected many swarms since then. The last three swarms I collected I managed not to collect a single sting. I just tell you so you don't make the same mistakes I did.

Wherever the swarm is, get your cardboard box close. Then, try and manipulate the center of the swarm into your box. You can gently scrape them with a piece of cardboard into the box. Or you can pick them up with your hands. What you are trying to do is get the queen into the cardboard box. The swarm will take all their clues from her. If you get her in the box, you can actually just wait patiently from there and the rest of the bees will slowly migrate into the box so they are close to her.

I don't much like waiting for the slow migration, so what I generally do is once I have the queen in the box, I begin to scoop handfuls of bees into the box atop the queen. Several hundred of the bees will begin to buzz loudly and will fly around bumping into you. They are warning you that they aren't happy with you. But you have your suit on—so don't sweat it too much. Just keep working slowly and after five or ten minutes, you will most likely have about 70% of the bees in the box. From there, just walk ten or twenty feet away from the box and wait a while. The rest of the bees will slowly settle down and land either where they were or in the box with the queen.

Now you have a decision. You can leave the bees that are not yet in the box in place and depart with your queen and her several thousand attendants that you already have boxed up, or you can try and get the rest. I feel it rather unkind to leave any bees behind. Left behind, they are sure to perish. So I generally spend as much time as I need to collect as many bees as humanly possible. Realize that you probably are never going to get them all. But, gather as many as you can. Thank the homeowner for the call. Tell them the few remaining bees will leave in the next three days and instruct them to just leave them alone until they depart. And then go home and put your bees in their new hive.

Can you depend on getting a swarm hive in a timely manner? Not really, it seems to happen when you least expect it. But in my world, a free swarm colony is welcome in my yard anytime I can get one. So for your first hive, I would purchase a packet of bees. But from there, if you get a call, why not go help your neighbor and get a free colony in the act of service. You will never believe how grateful the homeowners are when you leave with all those bees. A really thoughtful beekeeper would even take the homeowners a jar of honey as thanks for their call. Your gratitude will work wonders with them and you can certainly expect future calls from them or their friends if they ever get another swarm in their yard.

A note of caution. If the swarm in question is actually within the walls or roof of a house, I always defer to a professional removal service. There are just too many liability issues with trying to get bees out of a house. And the same goes if the hive is in a dangerous location such as too high in a tree. There is no shame in telling the homeowner you aren't set up to get that particular hive. Just help them call someone who can take care of it for them and head on your way.

You can also actively hunt bees by tracking them in flight and finding their home. I have never tried this. If you are interested, there is a book by John Vivian entitled "Keeping Bees" which has a fun chapter on tracking down beehives in the wild.

<u>Settling In</u>

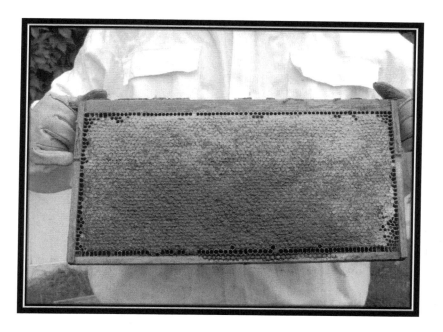

Welcome Home

You have all your hive equipment and are all ready to set up. You have picked your ideal location that gives your bees early morning sun and shade in the middle of the day. Now, to set up your hive.

First, put your piece of plywood or elevated hive stand down. If you aren't using one of these, skip this step. It isn't necessary, but either one will help your hive parts last longer.

Next, set your hive stand down. This step is important. Make sure the hive is as level as possible, with just the slightest of inclinations forward. This is to allow any moisture that builds up in the hive or gets into the hive to get out. A half inch incline from front to back should be plenty.

Place your bottom board down on top of the hive stand. On this, place one of your hive body boxes. These are the large boxes. Into the box, slide 9 or 10 frames. This part is your decision. Some beekeepers insist they get larger comb and more honey with just 9 frames. Others claim that 10 is the ideal number. I have used both and find no significant difference. So now, I just use 10 because that is what fits in the box exactly. If you decide to go with 9, you can do one of two things to space the frames perfectly. Some people purchase a tool that looks like an overlarge comb. It fits into the spaces between all the frames and spaces them perfectly. Others purchase a small metal insert for either end of the hive body box. These inserts have slots where you put the frames, thereby keeping the frames perfectly spaced. I do have one hive that still uses these. Mostly because I don't want to go through the hassle of taking them out. The colony is well established and I see no reason to disrupt their busy little lives. Other people who prefer 9 frames in their boxes just space their frames by eye.

If I were to do it over, I would just go with 10 frames in all my boxes. I'm definitely from the less hassle is better school of beekeeping. Ten frames fit exactly in the box. This makes it nice and easy.

Your next step is to place the next hive body on top of the first. Don't put your frames into this hive body. Now place your inner cover on your hive and your outer cover. Your hive is ready for homecoming. What about all the other parts? Those come into play later. Set them aside for now in a clean dry place. You will need them soon enough.

You get the exciting call that your bees are ready to pick up. If you ordered from a mail supplier, the call will come from the post office. If you ordered from a local supplier, they most likely will have let you know the day and time when you can pick up your bees. What next?

If you are going to pick your bees up, you have an exciting ride home awaiting you. I normally take a cardboard box with me. The box should be about 1.5 feet square or larger. When you arrive to collect your bees, they will be in a small shipping cage. The shipping cage will be roughly 12" long and about 6" deep and 6" wide. The top and ends are wood. The two long sides of the cage are a fine mesh. Inside the cage will be your "packet" of bees. To see 11,000 bees in such a small space is exhilarating. The top of the cage will have a can hanging down into the cage. It is a simple soup style can that hangs into the hole by the small lip around the edge of the can. On the bottom of the can, where you can't really see because the bees are covering it, is a hole with a mesh plug in it.

The can is full of sugar water and the extremely fine mesh allows the sugar water to drip out slowly, thus keeping the bees fed and watered during their journey.

Beside the can hole, on the top of the cage, you will see a small slot cut into the cage. Sticking up through the slot is a plastic tab that is stapled onto the top of the box. This plastic tab connects to the queen cage. She resides in a very small cage inside the larger cage.

So take the shipping cage and put it in the cardboard box you brought. There may be a few "loose" bees flying around your package of bees. Don't panic, they just want to be with their friends. They are very mellow right now and won't cause you any problems. Close the cardboard box and place it in your trunk or the back of your truck. Drive home. Smile with the happiness that comes from knowing you are now an official beekeeper.

When you arrive home, depending on your time schedule and the weather you can do one of a few things. If it is not the middle of the day, you can install your bees in their new home right away. If it is the middle of the day, or if you need to get some other things done first, the bees will keep ok for a few more hours in their shipping cage. If you are going to wait, do two things. Find a nice, protected and cool location for them. I put mine in the garage. Second, take a spray bottle and spray the hive down with some sugar water. No spray bottle? No big deal. Just use an old paintbrush and gently "paint" the mesh sides of the shipping cage with some sugar water. The sugar water will keep them cool and full while they wait. The bees will start to buzz a bit when you first do this, but they will mellow out quickly. They will definitely appreciate the extra food. Traveling is hard on all of us, the bees are no exception.

Let's jump ahead to the time you are ready to install your bees. The last thing you are going to need is either a marshmallow or a small amount of icing sugar mixed with water to make a thickish paste. Before you do the install, take a few moments to get acquainted with your new colony. Get comfortable with them, watch them, learn a bit about how they move and interact. It is amazing how much you can learn with some quiet observation.

Now it is install time. Get your bee gear on. Put on your bee suit, put on your gloves, grab your hive tool, and grab your marshmallow or powdered sugar paste. You are now ready for the install. To do this, you are going to need one extra tool. You can use both a hammer and a very small nail, or you can use a stapler. The large kind of stapler they use when installing carpet or for chores around the house, not the kind that is used in an office.

Grab the shipping cage and bring it over to where your hive boxes are waiting. Here are the steps you are going to take.

1. Remove the queen cage.

2. Remove the plug from the queen cage.

3. Install a candy plug in the queen cage.

4. Install the queen cage into the hive.

5. Remove the feeding can from the shipping cage.

6. Shake the bees into the hive.

7. Put the inner and outer cover back on the hive.

8. Sit down, grab a cold drink and relax. If you can arrange it, sit near your hive and watch the activity.

Now, let's go through these steps in a bit more detail.

First, remove the queen cage. How? Well, this part requires calm and steady hands. Most shipping cages come without a secondary cover, but yours may have a small cover atop the food can. If this is the case, remove the small cover. Now, slide your hive tool gently under the edge of the feeding can. Lift the feeding can about halfway out. Before you remove it totally, use your other hand to grab the plastic tab that holds the queen cage. It may be a thin metal tab. I have seen both. Wiggle it loose from the staple holding it down and hold onto it. You don't want to let go of this tab once you have it unstapled.

Now, pull the feeding can out of the shipping cage slowly and completely. As soon as it is clear, slide the tab down the slot it is in and pull it out from the large hole where the feeding can was. As you pull it out, you will notice a very small cage attached to the end of the tab. (Don't pull the tab in the up direction until it is out of the slot and into the hole where the can was—if you do, you may detach the queen cage which will lead to an exciting game of "reach into the pile of bees and find the tiny queen cage". I have played the game. Although not hard, it can be a bit exciting). As soon as the queen cage is clear of the shipping cage, gently set the feeding can back down into the hole. This will keep most of the worker bees in the shipping cage until you are ready for them. A few will fly out, just ignore them.

*If by chance you have decided to play a round of "find the

queen cage" don't worry. The bees are very docile right now. If the queen cage is dropped into the bee pile or becomes detached, gently reach in with one hand and begin to feel around for her small cage. As soon as you find it, slowly remove your hand. Once your hand is out of the shipping cage, take the queen cage in your other hand and then shake your first hand gently but firmly. This will detach the bees that are hanging onto your hand. Now, put the feeding can back in the shipping cage to keep the rest of the bees where you want them.

Second, take a moment to inspect your queen. Her cage is very small, just a few inches long and maybe an inch square. The small cage should have a cork or other plug in one end plugging the hole the queen is going to exit from. On either side of the cage is the some fine mesh. You are now going to install a "candy plug" in her cage. This will keep her in place in her tiny cage for a day or two while the colony acclimates to their new home. By the time the worker bees free her from her cage, her pheromones will be everywhere and the colony will feel right at home in the hive you have prepared for them.

So, get either a marshmallow or your icing sugar blend.

Gently pull the cork out from the hole. Replace it with a small piece of marshmallow or a dab of icing. Do these two steps almost as if it were one step. Pull the cork out with one hand and replace it immediately with your marshmallow or sugar paste using your other hand. You want to do this as quickly as possible because you don't want the queen to exit her little cage at this moment in time. Basically you want to "trap" the queen in her cage without making the new candy plug so thick it will be difficult for the worker bees to free her. I generally use about 1/3 of a small marshmallow. If I use icing I fill the small hole about 1/3 of the way down. Wait a minute for the icing to harden. Now, atop the queen cage there should still be the small plastic or aluminum strap. This takes you to the third step.

Take the small queen cage and open your hive. Take off both outer and inner covers. Now remove the top hive box—this box has no frames in it. Now remove one of the middle frames from the bottom box. This leaves a slot open. Now slide the queen cage gently down into the opening where the frame was. Tack or nail the plastic or aluminum strap onto the top bar of an adjacent frame. This should leave the queen hanging.

Make sure the queen cage has the mesh facing down the open slot, not towards the wax foundation. You don't want the mesh to be mashed up against the side of one of the adjacent frames. It could make it difficult for her to get food and water from the workers. Now that her cage is secure, insert the tenth frame back into the hive box and you are ready for the next step.

Replace the upper box, the one with no frames in it right now. Now grab your shipping cage full of bees and gently pull out the feeding can. Turn the shipping cage upside down over the hive box and give the shipping cage two or three sharp shakes. Your goal here is to shake the vast majority of the worker bees right down on top of the queen and her small cage. They will come out in large, buzzing clumps. The workers may buzz angrily for a moment or two but when they realize they are reunited with their queen, they will calm down quickly. Continue shaking the shipping cage until most of the bees are out. You aren't going to get them all out. It isn't worth the hassle. The bees still in the shipping cage are fine; they just aren't ready to move on with life yet. Leave them there and set them aside. Now, take a last quick look at your bees. Are they humming and happy? Good. Put the inner cover and outer cover back on the hive boxes.

Set the shipping cage with the recalcitrant bees that refuse to exit just outside the hive entrance. After a while, these bees will realize the rest of the colony has left and they will fly or crawl out of the shipping cage and move in with their sisters. They will smell the queen and move towards her. By morning, most of the bees will have exited the shipping container.

Now, grab a cold drink and set up a chair near your hive. Relax and enjoy a few moments with your bees. A few bees will be flying around. They are just checking out the locale.

Tomorrow or the next day, grab the small shipping cage and set it aside. Some local bee suppliers take a deposit on these shipping containers. If so, set it aside to take back next time you head over there. There may be a few dead bees in the cage or nearby. Don't worry, with that many bees there are bound to be a few that passed on to the great hive in the sky.

It has been a couple of days since you installed your bees and the queen into their new home. Are they okay? It is natural to wonder. Better yet, it is time to find out. So get out to your hive with all your protective gear. Fire up your smoker and put on your gear. When you are all set, smoke the hive gently. Just give your smoker a few slow pumps with the spout right near the entrance to the hive. You want the smoke to puff right into the hive. Now give the hive a minute or two to get the scent of the smoke. This isn't a kid's minute or two where they are back at you in about five seconds asking again, "Are we almost there yet?" No, this is a real minute or two.

After the wait, give your hive a more generous puff or three of smoke and then pull off the outer cover. There may be several bees sitting right there in the oval hole of the inner cover. Watch them carefully. If several of them stare at you and start humming or buzzing loudly, they are warning you to stay away. If this goes on, a few of them may fly out and bump into you. This ramming behavior is the next step in the progression of aggressiveness.

Don't let it go any farther than this. Give all those little bees that are perched on the edge of the inner cover hole a nice puff from your smoker. The buzzing will quiet down immediately and they will relax a bit. Now, lift up the inner cover gently. Most likely the cover won't be stuck down with propolis already, but if it feels stuck, gently insert your hive tool between the inner cover and the hive box. Now twist it slowly. You don't want to move fast or create a loud crack when you break the propolis seal free. Honey bees don't like loud sounds or fast movement.

After you remove the inner cover, you will be staring down into the upper box which still has no frames. Give the bees in the hive several vigorous puffs of smoke. Don't get it so close to them that the heat from the smoke hits them—that will hurt them. Just get the smoke moving in their direction. Often, with my smoker, the smoke is fairly clear. That is fine; it seems to be the smell of the smoke rather billowing clouds of smoke that gets them mellowed out.

Now, lift off the top box and set it to the side. Gently reach in and pull up the frame that has the small queen cage attached to it. If the queen is still in her cage, puff the bees with plenty of smoke, and then stick a small toothpick or other tool gently in the hole that is blocked with the candy plug. Try to remove most of the plug. Leave just a bit and then put the frame back in and close the whole hive back up. You will need to come back in two more days and do the next steps.

If the queen is free, gently loosen the queen cage and set it aside. Now, take a few moments to inspect the frame. If you can see the queen, great; if not, no big deal. Next, fill the upper hive box with the 9 or 10 frames. Whichever route you go is fine. Then set that box atop the lower box. Put on both covers and walk away. Your first hive inspection is done. Fantastic, you are now an experienced beekeeper.

Next step, the full inspection.

Spring: Busy as a Bee

There are several methods of beekeeping. I personally think they all are fine. It mostly depends on you and your preferences. Some people check their bees only occasionally. They fall in the "nature seems to have been doing just fine before me, I'm sure she will keep doing fine after me" camp. And then there are the people who are in the "I am quite certain I can help my bees succeed, together we will be the very best" camp. And, of course, there are people in between.

When I first started keeping bees, I checked my hives often. I checked them weekly. And then, after a few years, I realized that they did about the same whether I checked them or not. Now, I check them infrequently. Instead, I watch from the outside for visible clues as to the hive health. If things look good, I leave them alone. If things aren't going so well, I schedule the colony a visit with the Hive Doctor (that is me if you didn't guess).

But about ten days after installing a colony I like to check the hive fully. I want to make sure everything is okay with them and that they are taking to their new home. I also want to make sure the queen is doing well.

Here are the steps to checking your hive. You can do this as often as you feel prudent. But I would make sure to do it sometime after 10 days from hive install up to 21 days after the install. After that, you can keep checking weekly, every two weeks, once a month, or whatever you feel is best. I will tell you how I do it as well as what I look for. Every colony is a bit different and part of it is experience. As you work with your bees you will begin to get a sense of what a healthy colony does versus how a weak or sick colony acts.

Now, to check our hive. This is going to be an in depth inspection. We are looking for eggs, larvae as well as food supply. If possible, we would also like to see the queen.

Get your protective gear on. Get your smoker fired up. Take the first few steps just like you did when you removed the queen cage. Puff smoke in the front entrance. Wait one to two minutes. Puff some more smoke in. Lift the upper cover. Puff some smoke into the oval hole of the inner cover. Now remove the inner cover and being puffing smoke across the top of the hive. There may be many bees staring up at you. Give them all a gently smoke puff.

They will move back down into the hive. As you work this time around, every time you notice the buzzing getting louder or long lines of little bees lining up along the edge of a frame and staring up at you, give them a bit more smoke. This will help them stay mellow. This may be the most invasive inspection you will conduct on your hive for quite some time. So, make sure to pay attention to the bees and their behavior. If they start flying up and bumping into you, you need to smoke them more. If several of them are attaching to your clothes and stinging your clothes, you need to smoke them a bit more.

Now, remove the upper hive box and set it to the side. For this next step, I generally start at one end of the hive and work across the hive. This is where a frame hanger comes in very handy. Pull out one of the frames on the end. Most likely, there won't be anything on this frame. If there is, that is great—it means your bees are very, very busy. Now, set that frame on the frame hanger.

Work your way across the hive. Gently pull out each frame, one at a time. As you pull it out, hold the ends with both hands. This means you set your smoker down near you. I generally stick mine with the spout pointing almost into the hive entrance. This keeps a thin trail of smoke entering the hive. And if things get exciting, I can reach down and puff the smoker a couple of times, blowing extra smoke into the hive.

Hold the frame up and look at both sides. Is there any honeycomb being built? If there is, is there any nectar store in the honeycomb. The nectar will look like water in the comb. It may be fairly dark. Or it may be very light. Look at the bees on the frame. What are they doing? They most likely are busy working. Set that frame in the spot where the first frame was in the hive box. Remember, your first frame is hanging on the frame hanger, so there is a space in the hive body box where it was. Now inspect each frame carefully. The very outside two or three frames on either side will most likely have no wax and maybe just a few bees on them. Can you see the queen? She will be in the middle of a pocket of bees. A tell tale sign is that all the bees around her will be facing in—right at her. It will be like she is in the middle of a crowd of adoring fans. This is pretty much exactly what is going on. If you find her, watch her for a moment. It is always a special feeling to find the queen. Watch her to see if you can observe her laying eggs.

Now, as you inspect the middle frames, depending on how

long you have waited to do this inspection, you may see some honeycomb that is capped with wax. Most likely, this is brood waiting to hatch. Near the edge of the capped brood, you should see larvae. Working outwards from the larvae, you begin to see smaller and smaller larvae. When you get to the very edge, you may even be able to see the eggs. They are difficult to see unless you hold the frame just right. Hold the frame up in the air between you and the sun. Now, with the sun shining through from the other side, can you see tiny little rice shaped eggs in the bottom of the comb? If you can, those are eggs.

Outside the circular edge of brood and eggs, you may see a small, thin line of comb that is filled with pollen. The bees store it here so it is close for larva feeding. Outside of the pollen circle, you should see some nectar.

If everything looks good, you should have quite a few frames with comb on them. Probably between four and eight right now. Most of the inner frames should have at least a section with larvae or food. If so, things are going good. If not, don't get frustrated. Some colonies just get up and running a bit slower than others. Now, after inspecting each frame, slide the frames back to their original positions and stick the 1st frame you removed back in its spot.

Gently lift the upper hive box and stick it back on the lower hive box. Remember to keep smoking your bees. Now, inspect the upper box the same way you did the lower. Most likely, there will be fewer frames with anything on them in this box. If there is nothing yet, don't panic. It can take a while for the hive to get up to strength and get everything built up and filled.

Depending on how full the hive is, you have a decision to make. The decision has two different factors that affect it. First, if your colony is growing and things look good in the two hive body boxes, it may be time to put on your supers. Second, is the weather cooperating? The colony is still fairly young and may not be able to keep warm if you put super boxes on top. So, for me, if the nighttime lows are above 50° F and both the hive boxes have more than 4 frames mostly built out with honeycomb, then I will consider putting my super boxes on. If the night time lows are still below 50° F and/or the lower boxes still don't have 4 frames mostly built out with honeycomb, I will wait.

Now, after your full inspection, replace the inner and outer covers. Good job, you just completed your very first, full hive inspection.

How do you know if your colony is established? If it has been 60 days since install, your colony should be well established. Right when you install the bees, there are about 11,000. You don't get any new bees for at least 21 days. That is how long it takes if the queen lays some eggs the very first day in hive. During that first 21 days, your colony will actually shrink a bit. Some of the worker bees assigned to gathering resources will die. Some will be eaten by predators. By the time the first bees start emerging from their honeycomb birthing chambers, the colony could be as low as 6,000 to 8,000 bees. Then, over the next 30 days or so, the colony size begins to grow rapidly. If the queen has been laying around 2,000 eggs a day, the colony suddenly is getting nearly 2,000 new bees a day. In 30 days, this means the colony is 60,000 or more bees strong. So, after 60 days, your colony should be really humming along. Here are a few things you can look for from the outside of the hive to determine the health of the colony. These signs should be fairly good indicators of overall colony health.

First, watch how many bees are coming in and out of the hive entrance. When the temperature is moderate, between 60 and 85 degrees F, there should be a steady flow of bees into and out of the hive. If you watch for one minute, you should see roughly 40 bees or more land. As they land, their pollen baskets should be full. If you count much less than that, say 20 bees or so, it may be time to check the hive. Don't panic yet, it may just be an "off" minute you chose. Come back later and count again. Maybe even count again the next day. If the count seems consistently low, it could be that your queen isn't laying enough eggs or maybe she isn't laying at all.

Second, watch the behavior of the bees that are standing at the entrance. If they are lively and active, this means things are most likely good with the colony. They should approach many of the incoming bees. As they greet the incomers, they are checking for proper scents. If everything smells right, they let them in. If things don't smell quite right, maybe a stray bee has found its way into the wrong hive, they will begin to wrestle the bee out of the hive. You most likely won't see this action too often, but if you watch carefully, you may see it from time to time. Mostly, watch to make sure several bees are alert, active, and acting as sentries in the hive entrance.

Third, watch for bees imprinting. The first few months of the hive life and then again each spring this will be most noticeable. But you should see some imprinting happening almost all the time. The bees that haven't left the hive before come out and fly in front of the hive. They face the hive and fly up and down and from side to side. This imprinting, or orientation, flight can last for several minutes or even longer. From there, they often fly back down, land on the landing board and crawl back into the hive.

They may take another imprinting flight or not. But at any given time, you may see from two or three all the way up to fifty or sixty bees imprinting. The purpose of this flight is thought to imprint the visual cues of the hives location and appearance in the bee's minds. Then, when they return from longer flights, as they get close to the hive, they are able to pinpoint the exact right location to come in for landing. This is a fairly amazing feat. I have several hives within a couple of feet of each other. The bees rarely land in the wrong hive. All because of this orientation flight.

Fourth, look around the entrance of the hive. There may be a few dead bees, but there shouldn't be an excess. Normal would be under five or ten. More than that could be indicative of an issue with the hive. When a bee dies in the hive, a worker will pull the dead bee out and fly it away from the hive. The dead bee is generally deposited at a far enough distance from the hive that you won't see them. If there is an abnormal accumulation of dead bees in front of the hive, it could mean the workers are overloaded with dead bees and can't get them far enough away from the hive. It could also mean the workers are too weak to fly them much farther. Either way, it may be time to get in the hive and do an inspection.

The two exceptions to this rule are when your hive is brand new. In the first ten to twenty days, you may find more dead bees. Don't worry about it too much unless it seems there are several hundred. The other time you may find a whole lot of dead bees is right at the beginning of spring for those of you who keep bees in cold locations. During the winter, if the weather rarely or never gets above 50° F, you will have a buildup of dead bees in the hive. When it finally is warm enough for the bees to fly, they will be a bit overloaded with their dead and may just pile them up outside the entrance. Watch for this, if the hive entrance gets a bit clogged, you may want to open the hive and sweep out all the little carcasses. It will make things a bit easier on the workers in the hive. As a side note on this, I always tell my kids to wear shoes when they are on the lawn closest to the hive. Many dead bees get dropped on the lawn, and an unsuspecting person with bare feet can easily step on a dead bee and get "stung".

Fifth, watch carefully if a predator arrives. If a wasp, or beetle, or even ants try to wander into the hive, the bee's reaction should be swift. A battle should ensue and the bees should continue to pile into the fray until the battle is won. If there is little or no reaction to a strange visitor, it could mean the hive is weak and unable to protect themselves. Get in there and see what is going on.

Sixth, if the temperature is very hot, in the low to high 90's and even up into the 100's, watch for lots of bees coming out and fanning. There will sometimes be hundreds or even thousands of bees in a large "carpet" in front of the hive fanning their wings. Most likely they are just cooling the hive off. If this mass of bees keeps crawling up the front and then flying short distances before returning, you could have a potential swarm building. The appearance of pre-swarm activity and fanning are quite different.

If fanning, almost all the bees will be facing in the same direction and they will all be standing, buzzing their wings. In a pre-swarm, the bees will be moving a whole lot, they will be climbing up the front of the hive, sometimes even to the very top. From there, they will launch into flight only to come right back down to the entrance. If this is going on, go get your suit and gear ready. You may have a swarm on your hands and if you are quick, you may get a new colony. We'll talk about swarming a bit more later on.

Finally, watch for a laying worker or a queen that is unable to fertilize eggs. During an external hive inspection, you will know you have a laying worker if you see an abnormal number of drones. These problems don't arise often, but if they do you will want to fix them quickly to ensure optimal growth of the colony. A laying worker occurs when the queen dies and another queen doesn't take her place. Normally, the supersedure process goes off without a hitch. When a queen is not laying enough or there is some other issue with her, the workers will begin the process of raising a new queen to take her place. Sometimes, through the vagaries of nature, the new queen kills the old queen and then she herself dies, leaving the colony without a queen.

In this situation, a worker bee will occasionally step up and begin acting like the queen. There is one significant problem, she has not mated and because of this, her eggs will only hatch into drones. If you open your hive and there is no queen, there are lots of drones and you find several cells with multiple eggs in them, you have a laying worker. This situation is simply remedied but it will take a bit of work.

To rid yourself of the pesky laying workers you first need a new queen. Order a queen and when she arrives, take the following steps. During the day, when most of the older foraging bees are out collecting for the hive, move the entire hive about 150 feet away from where it was. To do this, you may need a hand truck or wheelbarrow. Once you have it there, open the hive and begin to remove every frame. Once you have all the frames out of the hive, inspect the hive box to ensure absolutely no bees are left in it. You can't even leave one.

Now, begin to remove all the bees from each frame. After you are sure there are absolutely no bees on a frame, it can go back in the hive box. If you allow even one bee to get back in, you may have just let in a laying worker and all your effort will be wasted. Once you have all the frames clean and no bees left in the hive at all, move the hive back to its original location. The nurse bees that were laying will not have taken an imprinting flight yet and will not be able to find their way back to the hive. All the foragers, when they return, are just fine because they weren't laying workers.

Now install your new queen as if it is an entirely new colony going into the hive. The returning foragers will take care of the new queen and soon enough, everything will be back on track.

As to the issue of an infertile queen, this happens very infrequently. If you notice that your hive has nearly no new brood, it could be your queen is either not laying or completely sterile. If this is the case, order a new queen. When she arrives, find and destroy the old queen. Install the new queen as if you were installing a brand new package of bees. Requeen the hive quickly if you suspect an issue with a queen, this will give you a better chance of a good honey harvest.

I sincerely hope you are having fun. The main point of beekeeping is to produce honey and wax. But for me, it is an enjoyable hobby as well. Spend time watching your bees. Study up on why they do what they do. As you learn about the bees, you will enjoy watching them even more. There are several wonderful books on beekeeping. Some of my favorites are the following:

1.   Keeping Bees by John Vivian

2. Hive Management by Richard E Boonney

3. A book of bees by Sue Hubbell

4. The Sacred Bee in Ancient Times and Folklore by Hilda M Ransome

5. The Hive and the Honey Bee (A Dadant Publication)

There are earlier versions of a similar book by Langstroth—the father of modern beekeeping, but I really like the Dadant version. It is nearly the end all, be all encyclopedia of bee knowledge. I use it often to look up questions or concerns that arise when I am working with my bees.

Is it Super Time?

When is it time to put supers on? And what are supers? The super is the hive boxes you put above the two hive body boxes. In these boxes, the bees store honey, the honey that you will harvest.

When is it time to put them on your hive? We have addressed this partially in an earlier chapter. But, realizing that there may be a bit of repetition here, I will address the entire issue of adding the supers onto your hive.

The first year I have a hive, I generally put the supers on as soon as the hive has 4 or more frames built out with honeycomb in both the bottom and top box of the hive, and the nighttime temperature stays above 50 degrees for several days in a row. The second condition isn't quite as important to me. I live in an area where the temperature fluctuates wildly. We may get two weeks of 60 degree weather during the days followed by three weeks of 80 degree weather followed by a week of 40 degree weather. So the first year, the build out of honeycomb in the hive boxes is the most important.

Subsequent years, I place my supers on my hive as soon as I can. If the daytime temperature is above 50 for 3 days out of 5, I will place my supers on my hive.

How many supers do you put on? As many of you remember, the bees will spend about 24 pounds worth of honey to build one pound worth of wax. So, if you put a bunch of brand new frames up above them, they may spend most of their energy building out wax honeycomb and never get enough food into the hive to store much excess honey. I generally don't put more than two medium super boxes on my hives. Sometimes I will put one large and one medium. If I were to use small boxes, I would probably use three.

Why do I need to get the supers on the hive? One, so you can start getting some delicious honey. And two, so your colony doesn't become cramped and start to prepare for a swarm. If your bee colony feels they are growing too fast and aren't going to have enough room for everyone, they are much more likely to swarm. If the bees feel there is plenty of room to stretch and grow, the instinct to swarm is dampened. For this reason, I try and get the supers on as early as possible.

When a hive swarms, you lose about 80% of the bees. Basically, a full size colony of 80,000 bees suddenly is back to square one with 15,000 bees or so. And a new queen. If you are lucky, when your hive swarms, you may get a "new" colony out of the deal, if you are able to catch the swarm. Your colony that remained behind will be small. It will take that colony about a month to get back to full strength. And a small colony isn't going to collect much nectar on your behalf. There are just too few bees to get the job done. So, anything you can do to prevent swarming is a good thing. The easiest, and in my experience most impactful, thing you can do is to get your super boxes on early enough so the colony feels like it has more than enough room.

Later in the season, when the cold is beginning to be felt in the air, the bees are much less likely to swarm. They seem to instinctually know that there isn't enough time for a new hive to get established and will resist swarming. So if things get cramped later in the season it isn't quite as critical. But, if you are inspecting your hive, and the supers you have on the hive are getting nice and full, feel free to add another. It can't really hurt, and who knows, you may get a few extra pounds of honey out of the deal. Throughout the summer months, my rule of thumb is that if both (or all three if you are using three) super boxes are 80% or more full of capped honey, I will add another super box to the stack.

The Bee Days of Summer

Swarming happens. Although most beekeepers wish it would never occur, the bees have an evolutionary tendency, like all living creatures, to continue the species. Swarming is their natural instinct in response to various situations that the colony "views" as potentially threatening to the continuation of the species. When they swarm, the hive is continuing the life of the hive by splitting it into two separate hives. Think of it as the reproduction of the hive as opposed to the reproduction of an individual bee.

Swarming seems to happen for the most part during late spring or early summer. In each area of the country, there will be a time that occurs after the hard season of overwintering where the first spring pollens and nectars are available. After this first rush of food and warmth, most areas have a slight drop in the availability of food sources. This mini season of lack lasts anywhere from 4 to 6 weeks and can happen at different times in different area. But in your area, it will most likely be fairly consistent from year to year.

During the rapid increase in food sources in early spring, the queen begins to lay heavily. She is preparing her colony for maximum size during the best collection months of spring, summer and early fall. Three weeks after the beginning of this egg laying activity, as expected, there is a sudden and rapid growth in the number of bees in the hive. This sudden growth in colony size is accompanied by various other events.

If the colony is to swarm, to replicate itself for the continuation of the species, now is the time when the small preparations will begin to happen. First, as the queen is in this egg laying frenzy, the worker bees may prepare between 6 and 12 queen cells for future queens. They may begin to do this in response to overcrowding (which is solved by adding supers) or in response to the sudden drop in food sources.

The workers, reacting to adverse conditions, feed these special future queens only royal jelly. About a week before these new queens are to hatch, you may notice an abnormal number of bees hanging out on the bottom of the hive. There may be so many that they even spill out onto the front landing area. They don't seem to be doing much, just resting. They are preparing for the division of the colony and the swarm flight. The day or two before the actual swarm event, which will be a few days before the first of the future queens emerges from their cells, the bees that are to leave with the swarm begin to engorge themselves with honey. This is the food storage they take with them to start the new hive. At this same time, several scouts may be sent out to begin looking for a future hive location.

Then, on the day of the event, a couple of bees begin to do a special dance called the "whir" dance. After a few moments, dozens of other bees join in this dance. The dance gets the entire hive excited into a buzzing, frenzied mass. Suddenly, they burst forth from the hive in a frenzied flight of thousands. The number of bees that leave with the swarm can be over 30,000 and generally represent anywhere from half to three quarters of the hive's population. This flying frenzy is quite a sight to behold. If you haven't ever witnessed it, it is one of nature's majestic events.

Although the bees can be somewhat disconcerting to people who witness the event, in actuality, they are at their least defensive and are quite unlikely to attack or sting. Most of them are stuffed full of honey and just want to get to their new home. They will fly a short distance and settle somewhere, waiting to hear back from the scouts. Once the scouts find the best location, the mass will take off again and fly to their new home.

There is even a chance you will have several swarms in a row from the same hive. The original queen leaves with the first and largest group of bees. The first virgin queen that emerges from her queen cell may just up and leave with a secondary group of swarming bees. As soon as she finds a new home, they will settle, she will mate and the colony will begin to grow. The second virgin queen that hatches in the original hive now faces the same choice. If the original colony was extremely large, she may leave with a third group. These after-swarms get smaller and smaller. Eventually, one of the hatching queens decide to stay in the original hive. She finds all the other queens that are about to hatch from their cells and quickly kills them in their cells by stinging them to death. Now she rules supreme. In the next few days, she will mate and then begin to lay.

Because the loss of bees is so large when a hive swarms, the colony that is left behind can take four to six weeks to get back to size. This drop in size generally correlates with a drop in the amount of honey your hive will produce. For this reason, the beekeeper, for the most part, wants to prevent swarms. This can be done in a variety of ways. You may do every single one of these preventative efforts and your hive may still swarm. Sometimes, nature cannot be stopped no matter how hard we try. But as long as you give it your best effort, that is all that can be asked of the diligent beekeeper.

The first step to prevent swarming behavior is to make sure the colony has plenty of space. This needs to be balanced carefully with the overall health of the colony. If your weather is cold, and the bees have a very large area to try and keep warm, they will suffer. But, if the weather is suddenly warm, and the bees feel there isn't enough future space, they may begin their preparations for swarming. And so, your goal is to identify the earliest possible time you can place super boxes on top of your hive without causing the colony to suffer excessive cold.

I live in an area where the early spring weather is entirely unpredictable. One day it may be 70 degrees and the next the highs might be 20 degrees. So, what I do, is wait until there are three or four days of warm weather (days with the high above 50) in a row and then I check the future weather forecast. If the weather isn't supposed to drop precipitously in the next three to five days, I place my super boxes on that very day. If the weather is going to drop, then I wait. After it warms back up for three or four days, I check the weather forecast again. I keep doing this, until I have the chance to place the supers on the hive. The earlier the better. More space means a happier colony.

The second thing to do is to switch the two hive body boxes once in the early spring and then again in the late spring. Doing this helps the hive create the largest brood area possible. It only takes a few moments and is amazingly beneficial to the future growth of the colony as well as helping to reduce the chance of a swarm. Just open the hive. Remove the supers if they are already on the hive. Pull off the top hive body box. Remove the lower. Put the top hive in the spot where the lower hive box was and then put the lower box on top of the upper. Reassemble everything. Then about six weeks later, repeat this process so the two hive body boxes are back in their original positions.

The next thing I do is I check the hive every two weeks from the end of April until the end of June. These are very quick checks looking for just a couple things. One, I am looking for capped brood. If there is plenty of capped brood, it means the queen is busy at work. Two, I am looking for queen cells. If there are any, I carefully scrape them out of the hive. If you prevent new queens from getting even close to hatching, then your hive will not swarm. This is a tough route to go, because if you do it, you need to make sure you find each and every queen cell in the hive. If you miss even one, the hive can still swarm. These queen cells are sometimes referred to as swarm cells. If you see them, you most likely will see 6 to 12 of them. Scrape these off and hope for the best. If you do scrape them off, you need to check at least every 10 days to 2 weeks for more. The bees may keep trying to produce more queens.

Finally, if you are extremely worried about swarming, you can take these precautionary steps. It seems that high temperatures can incite swarming. Your bees need plenty of water and air so they feel cool. Make sure there is a source of water close to your bees. An easy way to provide this is fill a flower pot base with several layers of stones or marbles. Then fill it with water. The marbles or stones should protrude above the level of the water. This provides the bees with an easy place to stand while they get water.

To increase hive circulation you can drill a few holes in your upper hive body. Just drill four to six holes in the body. When it is hot, leave the holes open. In the fall and winter, plug the holes with a small dowel, a cork or even duct tape. This allows the hive to get plenty of fresh air when things are hot. The cool air will reduce their desire to swarm.

If your hive seems determined to swarm, you can take one final, more drastic step. You can split the hive. Generally this step will stop the original colony from swarming and you will end up with two smaller hives. But, with a few weeks time, they will get back up to strength and you may even end up with more honey than you started. How do you split the hive?

Just take these few easy steps and you will have it done. First, make sure you have all the boxes and frames and other hive pieces you need for your "new" hive. Your new hive needs to be set up at least six feet away from the old hive, preferably a bit more than that. Set up that hive with six frames in the bottom hive box and either nine or ten in the top hive box. Leave the four middle spots open in the bottom. Now, smoke your original hive and open it up.

For this step, you need to find the old queen. To do this, you are going to take out each of the frames in the bottom hive box, one by one. As you remove each one, check it carefully. She will be quite obvious once you find her, but sometimes the search can be frustrating. Look for her extra large body and several bees in a circle around her. Once you find the queen, carefully check the frame she is on for any queen cells. If there are any, you need to scrape them off. Then put this frame in your new hive. Right in the middle. Next, pull out one more of the frames with lots of capped brood on it. Make sure there are no queen cells on this frame either. You don't want your new hive to have a queen and a future queen. While you are doing this, you need to find at least one frame with a queen cell or two on it—make sure this frame stays in the original hive.

Now, if everything is done right, you have two frames of brood cells and the queen in the new hive, with absolutely no queen cells. In the old hive, you should have one or more frames of brood as well as at least two or three queen cells. Now pull two frames from the old hive that are on the outside. These should have no brood in them but should have some honey, nectar and pollen. Put these in your new hive. Try and shake about half the bees into the new hive. You can do this by lifting out frames covered in bees and then shaking them once, very firmly above the new hive frames.

The bees will fall off and into your new hive. Once you have roughly half the bees in the new hive, close it up with frames in each spot. Put your queen excluder on, add at least one super if not both. And now put the top on. This new hive should be ready to go. Treat it like a brand new hive and go through each of the steps you normally would with a new hive.

Now close up the original hive and treat it like a new hive as well. But with this one, give it a couple weeks before you start getting into it. This will give the new queen time to mate and get busy with laying eggs.

No matter what you do, sometimes a hive will just swarm. If yours does, try and follow their original path. Most likely they will come in for a landing somewhere within a quarter mile of their starting spot. If you can track the swarm to its first landing spot, then you have a good chance of collecting a free colony. At least if you do catch it, it takes some of the sting out of losing half your hive to a swarm.

Harvest and Beyond

Harvest the Liquid Gold

Getting ready for the harvest is exciting. The harvest stands as the culmination of several months of work on your part and thousands upon thousands of flights by your bees. As you prepare for the harvest, there are a few tools you are going to need.

Here is the quick list of what you must absolutely have:

1. Honey Extractor
2. Uncapping knife
3. Uncapping fork
4. Honey Strainer
5. Bottling bucket
6. Containers to store your honey

There is no reason you need to go out and buy all these pieces of equipment. Many bee stores around your area will most likely rent them to you for a nominal charge. Even better, find another beekeeper in your area and ask them what they use. If they have their own, offer to pay if they will let you use it for a weekend. Most likely they will be happy to share the cost. When I first started, I couldn't find anyone around to share harvest equipment with, so I purchased my own extractor. It was a fairly substantial investment at the time, but since then it has been used hundreds of times by many people.

What does each piece of equipment do?

The extractor is a large stainless steel barrel with a handle at the top. Inside, you will find a pair of cages attached vertically to the center bar. Your hive frames slide down into these cages. The handle spins the center bar. As you spin the handle, the frames are spun rapidly inside the barrel which flings the honey out of the frames using centrifugal force.

The uncapping knife is a large, flat bladed affair that plugs into a socket. The electricity heats it up. You use this knife to slice across the tops of the frames removing the caps of wax in the process. They are handy items, but if you are only extracting one hive or even two, you can probably get away without one. Instead of an uncapping knife you can also just use an uncapping fork if you are just extracting a couple of hives.

An uncapping fork is just a small tool with multiple tines that are used to scratch the caps off the stored honey. Some people just use these for the spots they can't reach with the uncapping knife. On small extraction jobs, you could reasonably just use the fork without an uncapping knife. Once or twice, in a pinch, I've even just used a kitchen fork for the entire uncapping process.

The honey strainer comes in many different forms. My extractor actually sits on a lower stainless steel drum that catches all the honey as it comes off the frames. As it passes from the upper area to the lower area, it also passes through a finely meshed steel strainer. This catches out all the small pieces of wax and debris that seem to invariably try to get into the honey.

From there, I pour my honey through another, even more fine strainer into my bottling bucket. A bottling bucket is just a five gallon bucket with a spigot at the bottom. Once full, you just turn the spigot and out comes honey ready for final containers.

The honey containers you use can be anything from four ounce glass jars all the way up to five gallon buckets and beyond. Some years I buy several hundred plastic honey bears with squeeze lids and put all my honey into those. I use small glass jars to bottle honey for local sales. And I put many pounds of honey into quart jars for my family storage needs.

How do you tell when your honey is ready to be harvested? If you open your hive and the top supers are full of honey, it is time to harvest. I have had this happen as early as July and as late as October. The way to tell if your super is full is to see how many frames have capped honey in them. As the season progresses, your bees will busily store honey in the super frames. As the unripened honey turns to ripe honey, the bees will cap it with some wax to maintain it at the appropriate moisture level. Honey is hygroscopic, which means it will absorb moisture from the surrounding air. If you live in an area with high natural humidity, the caps keep the honey from absorbing moisture and changing into not honey.

The bees seem to always start filling the frames starting near the middle. As the season goes on, the frame will slowly hold more and more capped cells that are full of delicious honey. Once a super has 7 or 8 frames that are about 85% capped, it is time to extract the honey. Another way to tell if it is full is to do the lift test. Simply lift the super box. If a large super feels like it weighs over 50 pounds, then it is probably close to being ready. I normally lift them until they feel the right weight. This is less invasive for the bees. Once I think they are about the right weight, then I get in and check the individual frames to make sure they are about 85% capped.

Remember, the bees are going to need food through the winter, so unless you plan on eliminating your hive, never take honey from the two lower hive body boxes. Your bees need between 50 and 70 pounds of honey to make it through the cold season. If their lower boxes are full of capped honey cells, they have plenty. The bees always seem to work outward and upward. So rest assured, if your supers have plenty of capped honey, your main body will most likely have plenty as well.

When you do your regular inspections, check the upper super boxes. When you notice that they are about 85% capped, the time has arrived. I wait for this 85% full event or until the last week of September. Whichever comes first, that is my signal to extract honey. I don't wait into October because in my area the weather generally turns cold in October making the honey more viscous and difficult to extract.

The big day has arrived. It is time to extract your honey. There are many possible ways to do this, but I am going to share the steps I take. After several years of trial and error, this seems to work best for me. If you want to go another route, then by all means, try another way. If it works out well for you, feel free to share your success with me on my website, www.UrbanHomesteadBooks.com.

First, get prepared, by making sure you have your bee suit, you smoker, plenty of fuel for your smoker (because today is going to be a longer session with the bees than your average inspection), and your bee tool.

You also need to have an extractor ready, which can be fairly expensive to purchase. So if you can find someone that will lend you one or even rent you one for a few days, that is a good route to go when you are first getting started. Once you have several hives and know exactly what you like and want, you can pick up your own extractor and then share it or even rent it to others.

You are also going to need somewhere to keep all your golden harvest. I put mine in Mason quart jars. They store easy, they seal well, and they have just the perfect size for whatever you plan on doing with your honey. I always put some of my honey in small pint jars to use as gifts for family and friend gifts. Most of them return the jars and this lets me know when they need more.

You are also going to need a few other things—these are listed under the Extraction Tools section in the Gearing Up section of this book. You are going to need an uncapping knife and/or an uncapping fork, an extraction tank, a stainless steel strainer, a honey bucket with gate valve, and a brush. There are bee brushes, but I don't love them. I just went to a local hardware store and bought a small hand broom/brush that is about 12 inches long and has nice soft bristles. You will also need an extra super box with no frames in it, you can substitute a myriad of things for this, but a super box is easiest. One year I used a cardboard box and it was just fine.

Now that you have all your gear assembled, get your suit on and let's go outside and get started.

My first year, I thought I would be extra humane and use some scent to chase the bees off the frames. They sell special scent to chase the bees off the frames. You can purchase it from any beekeeping supply store. It was an utter disaster that took about three hours longer than it should have. If you want my advice, the easiest way to get your honey frames ready for extraction is the quickest and the least invasive on the hive. So here is what to do.

Pick which hive you are going to work with first. Start your smoker and smoke the hive a bit. While you wait for the bees to do their thing, place your extra super box nearby on a flat spot of ground. I normally place it about five to ten feet away from the hives. Then, smoke your hive a bit more and take off the top super. Set it on the ground about two feet from the hive. Then take off the next super (if you have two on your hive main boxes) and set it on top of the first super. If you have three, take it off and stack it up with the other supers as well. Now, place your hive top back on the, now, much shorter hive. This will keep the majority of the bees from coming out to inspect your work.

Now that the hive is taken care of, move over to the supers. There will be several if not several hundred bees flying around the supers. Just ignore them. Pull out a frame from the end of the super box. If you need to loosen any propolis stuck frames, the hive tool does a bang up job of this. Pull the frame out and move over so you have the frame right in front of the hive and give it a big shake. Not a side to side shake. Just take the frame in your two hands and lift it about chest high. Now move it quickly towards the ground. When you have the frame about a foot or two above the ground stop your downward movement suddenly. The quick jerking motion will dislodge nearly all the bees into a pile right in front of the hive.

It doesn't hurt them, it puts them right on their doorstep and it gets your frame nearly clear of bees. Now take your frame and brush the remaining bees off with quick, firm sweeps of your hand broom. Here is why you want soft bristles on your broom. Hard bristles break the caps on the honey and the honey starts to leak out. Just whisk the bees off both sides. Take long, firm strokes to sweep the bees off. Don't let your strokes be short, jabbing affairs. That will only serve to antagonize the bees. Once you have the frame clear of bees, set the bee free frame over in your empty super box.

Continue doing this with this super until you have all the frames from the super you are working on bee free and in the spare super box. Now, take the newly filled super box and set it in your house on some newspaper or an old towel. This will keep curious bees from coming to take the free honey. Go back out to your hives and use the now empty super box as your "to be filled" box and start the process over with the next super box.

Do this with each frame until you have all the frames done. When you are done with your first hive, just step over to your next hive and start the process over. Quick and easy, the whole process shouldn't take much over 20 to 30 minutes per hive. Once done with all your hives, it is time to move on to the fun part of the day.

Go inside, get a nice drink of water and rest a couple of minutes.

All rested? Good. Now set up your extractor if you haven't already. Near it, place your extraction tank. My extraction tank, you ask? It is simply a 9 x 13 Pyrex pan. My extractor has a tank below it where it catches all the honey. Between the main body and the lower holding tank there is a fine, stainless steel mesh strainer that catches most of the debris. There will always be a bit of debris coming out of the frames. Things like small pieces of wax, honeybee wings, and maybe even a bee or two. If yours is similar, great. If not, at some point you are going to need to move the honey through a fine, stainless steel strainer to get out the stuff you don't want.

An uncapping knife will make things go faster, but if you only have just a few hives to extract, you can actually make do with just an uncapping fork. If yours is an electric knife, plug it in and wait a few minutes. When it is hot, take your first frame and run the knife down the frame from bottom to top. Hold the knife at about a

35 degree angle to the frame. Don't force the knife, the heat will melt the caps and they will come off fairly quickly. Just move the knife across the surface slowly but firmly. Once you have uncapped both sides, quickly place the frame into your extractor. I have a small extractor that holds just four medium frames or two large frames. Some are even smaller, some larger.

If you are extracting with just an uncapping fork, just pull the fork across the entire surface of capped honey on each side. You need to be firm with this. Make sure you pull off all the caps. This method is a bit rougher on the remaining honeycomb, but the bees fix it all up later.

Once your extractor is full with two, four or even more frames, close the lid and get turning—if yours is a manual labor style like mine. Spin your extractor moderately fast for about a minute. Now, reach in and flip all your frames so they are facing the opposite way.

Begin to spin again. As you spin your extractor this time, the first minute or two will go fairly easy. Suddenly, it will seem very hard to spin. Keep spinning. As the exercise nuts say, push through it. After 30 seconds to a minute of this heavy feeling, the extractor will suddenly spin much more freely. This means the majority of the honey just spun out of the frames. An extractor, as you most likely guessed, works on centrifugal force. As the frames spin, the honey slowly is pulled out of the honeycomb cells. As the pressure builds, right before the vast majority of the honey flies out, the extractor becomes very hard to spin.

Keep spinning for another minute or so while it is easy to spin. Then, stop your extractor. Reach in and flip your frames one more time. Spin it again for another minute or two—until it is very easy to spin. By now, your frames should be empty. Take them out and set them back in the super box.

Extract your remaining frames the very same way.

Once you are done, it is time to bottle the honey. Make sure your honey has gone through a fine stainless steel strainer at least once. As I said earlier, my extractor is two parts. The upper part is a stainless steel drum with the spinning mechanism and the lower part is a holding tank. My holding tank has a gate valve. I just put the holding tank up on my counter and run all the honey out of it into a five gallon bucket with an extremely fine nylon mesh strainer in the top of it. Once the five gallon bucket is full, I set this on the counter and begin to fill the individual Mason jars from it. The honey that goes into the jars has been twice strained and is ready for storage, eating, baking, selling and anything else you want to do with it.

A cautionary note. Unpasteurized honey will blow your mind. It has flavor beyond any honey you have ever tasted before. It tastes even more delicious because your bees made it. But, unpasteurized honey can also contain botulism spores. It is highly unlikely but still possible to get sick from unpasteurized honey, which is exactly what your freshly extracted honey is. So never give this honey to anyone under the age of one or anyone who may have a compromised immune system. Also, if you sell your honey or give it away, you should include a warning to this effect. You don't want anyone to get sick.

If you are going to brand and sell your honey, get some nice stickers for whatever bottles or jars you are going to sell it in. Make sure they look attractive and include any required nutritional information as well as a clear warning about unpasteurized honey. If your bees aren't in an area where the only flowers they can access are a single kind (such as clover, lavender, etc) then your honey is considered wildflower honey. Mark it as such. Your customers are going to love it just as much as you do.

Get Them Ready for Bed: Fall Management

For your bees to survive through the winter, they need adequate food storage. If your bees run out of honey, the entire colony will die off. If they run out of pollen, they will not even attempt to raise brood in the spring. How much honey and pollen do you need for the winter?

The answer depends on where you live. If you live in bitter cold areas such as the far Northeast or the very northern part of the Midwest, your hives will most likely need 80 or more pounds of honey. If you live in a climate with mild winters, it could be your hive will only need 50 pounds or even less.

To determine how much honey your hive has available you will need to do an inspection. Open up your hive and lift the individual frames out. Each frame full of honey has about 5 pounds of honey in it. So if you live in a cold area, you need about 14 of these full frames available for your bees. If it looks like your bees don't have enough, you can assist them before winter hits.

When the ambient temperature doesn't get above 50° F, the bees won't leave the hive. If the weather stays below this temperature for an extended period of time, you want your bees to have enough food. Where I live, winter (by which I mean extended periods where the temperature doesn't ever rise above 50° F) generally starts to kick in by the beginning of November. So at the beginning of October I check my hives. If they have enough food, then this part is done with. If they are a bit shy on food reserves, I set out some sugar water for them to collect. This is easy to mix up. Boil 2.5 quarts of water. Once it is boiling, turn off the heat. Now add 10 pounds of white granulated sugar to the water. You don't want the heat going once the sugar hits the water. The sugar will caramelize which can make your bees sick. Stir the sugar until it is all dissolved. Now just allow the water get to room temperature. Set it right next to your hive or put it in your hive feeder (if you have one) once it is cooled. The bees will eat it up and make it into honey. In fact, this recipe will give the bees about 12.5 pounds of stored honey. So if you know your hives need more than this, mix up a couple of batches. Before you mix them up and give them to the bees, read the next section on medication. You can add the medication right to the mixture and get a few chores done at once.

While the honey made from sugar water is indistinguishable from honey produced from nectar, it is not ok to try and boost your honey production in the spring and summer using sugar water. In fact, in most areas it is against the law. But for your bees' winter food stores, it is just fine. My rule is as long as there are no upper supers on my hives, I can feed my bees sugar water if necessary be it spring, summer, fall or winter. Once the upper supers are on, no more feeding the bees.

A pollen shortage is a whole other issue. If your hive has 3 to 5 frames with lots of pollen on them, your hive is just fine. In the late spring and early fall, the bees naturally try and collect and store extra pollen. For some reason, sometimes they fail to do so. If your hive has little to no pollen, don't panic, just make a note of which hive is short on pollen. In the early spring, you can feed them pollen or a pollen substitute which will get them going just fine. Why not give them the pollen in the fall? They won't take it and it will just go to waste.

Do your bees need medicine? Once again, it depends on your individual hives. I prefer to give my bees as little medication as possible, but there are some medications you should administer to your hive on a regular basis. You must medicate against foulbrood. Terramycin is used for this. You should also medicate for nosema, which is an intestinal disease bees can get. You can treat this with Fumidil B. Both are available online or from a local bee supply store. When you mix up your fall sugar water, you can just add both of these to the mix. Follow the directions on the packages as to amounts. I'll talk a bit more about bee diseases in a later chapter. For now, just rest easy knowing these are the only two medications that you really need to give your bees regularly. Other medications can be administered regularly or just when needed. You can find all the information you need about this in the chapter on Diseases, Pests and Other Problems.

There are several things which can adversely affect your hive through the winter. They include excess moisture, carbon dioxide build up, heavy winds, extreme cold snaps, extremely long cold spells and pests. Harm to your hive from these issues can be easily prevented with just a bit of planning and work. Let's tackle the issues.

Excess moisture and carbon dioxide build up. During the

winter, the hive will cluster. When the temperature drops, the bees clump together in a winter cluster. The worker bees surround the queen bee and keep her at just the right temperature. As the temperature drops more, the bees cluster more tightly. When it heats up a bit, the cluster gets a bit looser. The whole time the bees are in a cluster, they are rotating positions from the outside to the inside and back again. Only the queen stays right in the middle, nice and toasty warm.

This big ball of breathing bees creates two things, moisture and carbon dioxide. As they breathe in and out, their breath slowly builds up condensation inside the hive. As this condensation collects into small droplets, it can drip down on the hive cluster making things rather uncomfortable for the bees. Too much build up can be fatal to the cluster. During this same process, carbon dioxide is created. Too much can also be fatal to the hive, the easiest way to prevent both is to make sure there is adequate ventilation in the hive.

There are several ways to do this. Some beekeepers put an insulation board between the inner cover and the top hive body box. This insulation cover gives extra protection against the cold and allows both the moisture and the carbon dioxide to escape before they build up inside the hive. Another group of beekeepers glue a small wooden stick on each of the inner cover's four corners. Small pieces of Popsicle stick works just great. These glued on pieces of wood create a razor thin air space between the hive body and the inner cover allowing moisture and carbon dioxide to escape. Either method works great. If I was in a really cold area, I would probably use an insulation board because it will also prevent moisture and carbon dioxide build up and keep the hive a bit warmer.

Next is the issue of heavy winds. Bees don't like the cold blowing up their skirts, so to speak. If your area is prone to heavy winds, find a way to create a wind break in front of the hive. Anything will work; you could even put a large planted pot in front of the hive. Just keep it a few feet from the entrance of the hive and it will work as an adequate wind break. Doing so will keep your bees happy and warm.

Extremely long periods of cold or extreme cold snaps can both be dangerous to your bees. By extremely long periods of cold I mean three weeks or more where the temperature doesn't get much above 40° F or where the temperature is below 0° for a few days straight. I live in hardiness zone 5 and have never needed to do this extra step. But if you live in a colder area, you might need to take precautions. Both of these issues can be resolved the same way. If you expect either issue in your area, just wrap your hives in tar paper. A single or double layer should be plenty. You can tack it lightly right to the box with a staple gun to keep it on through the winter. Just make sure you put holes in the tar paper to match the holes in the hive where the bees need to get out. The black tar paper will absorb heat and keep your hive a bit warmer. It should be plenty.

The final issue is mice. In the winter, mice like to stay warm, just like you and I do. For some, the lure of a nice warm beehive is just too much and in they go. The bees will mostly leave them alone, but the mice may wreak havoc on your hive parts and chew up unprotected honeycomb. Plus they aren't the cleanest animals in the world. If you are nervous about mice in your area, you can purchase a mouse guard that fits right over the hive opening. Or you can just tack some 3/8" mesh wire over the opening. This will let the bees in and out but will prevent the mice from trying to overwinter in the hive. If you decide to use a mouse guard, make sure to remove it every couple of weeks and remove any dead bees. If you don't, the dead bees will build up to unhealthy levels. Normally bees will remove their own dead, but sometimes with a mouse guard in place they have trouble getting them out of the hive. Help your little workers out with regular checks.

Winter Time: A Time to Plan

What are your little bees doing through the winter? Mostly the same as you. Eating and keeping their loved ones warm. During times where the temperature drops below 50° the bees will form a cluster. This cluster keeps the core temperature (the temperature in the middle of the cluster) at a nice, steady 92° F. This ensures the queen is warm and safe. The other bees continually move about within the cluster. When they get too cool, they slowly work their way into the middle. When they are too hot, they move out to the edges. Each of them taking turns on the outer fringes.

The bee's metabolic rate slows through the winter and they consume less food. While they are clustered together, they will form a tighter ball when it is colder and loosen up when it is warm. Occasionally, when there are extended periods of extreme cold, the cluster will not loosen up and the colony can actually starve to death. You see, when the cluster is loose, it is able to move slowly over to food stores that are one or two frames away. When the cluster is very tight, it won't move through the inside of the hive. Because they won't move, the colony can actually starve to death even though there is available food just one frame away from where they are located. This phenomenon is known as cold starvation. To best prevent this, if you live in an area with extended periods of extreme cold, make sure you wrap your hives in tar paper. The extra heat generated will be just enough for the bees to loosen up and move over to get more food.

The bees will not defecate in the hive. If you see some in the hive it can be a sign of sickness and you need to inspect your hive carefully. Because the bees don't fly when it is cold, they just "hold it". As soon as the weather warms up to 50° F, the bees will come storming out and let it all go. If you go outside some sunny winter morning and see your snow covered with yellowish brown spots and a few dead bees, don't worry, it is just the girls finally getting their chance to relieve themselves. The few dead bees are just from a bit of housekeeping they do while they have the chance.

You actually don't have any winter chores except to check on the hives every week or two. I normally go out and knock on the side of each hive. Then I listen carefully. If I hear the bees begin to buzz their protest to my noise, it means they are alive and well.

While I am there, I check the entrance quickly to ensure there isn't a buildup of dead bees. If there are any, I quickly sweep them out without opening the hive.

Then, in the late winter and early spring I begin to check the hive for adequate food supplies. To do this, wait for a reasonably warm day. Make sure there are a few bees out flying. Then, suit up and quickly peek inside the hive. Don't pull out any of the frames, but look down in between them. You are looking to see if there is capped honey. If it seems they have a few frames with capped honey, then all is good. If not, you may need to mix up some sugar water and get it to them.

This is a good time to feed pollen to the hives that failed to store up any before winter. You can just sprinkle pollen inside the hive. Or, if you would rather, mix some of the pollen or artificial pollen with some 2:1 sugar/water mix until you have a stiff patty of the stuff. Just stick this patty right on top of the frames inside the inner cover. The bees will eat it up and be delighted. This will get them going, and encourage the queen to begin laying eggs for the spring build up.

If you do need to begin feeding a hive, you MUST continue

to feed the hive until you see them collecting their own pollen and nectar in the spring. The extra food availability will stimulate the colony to get into action. Brood will be reared and the bee population will quickly explode. If you quit feeding them before they are bringing in their own food, they will swarm or die off and you will lose the colony.

Other than these few chores, the rest of the winter should be spent enjoying time with your loved ones. Visit friends and family you haven't seen in a while. Take them a jar of honey or a pair of beeswax candles. Laugh and smile. This is the season of rest. Spring will be here soon, so make sure to take full advantage of your free time.

Second Year and Beyond

The second year, and subsequent years, have a different pace to them. There are a few things which need to be taken care of in the late winter and early spring that weren't necessary the first year because you hadn't hived your colony yet. Let's review what things should be done in the late winter and early spring for your bees.

First, you should go out on a warmish day and knock on the side of the hive. If you hear buzzing, your bees are probably ok. As soon as you have a sunny day above the 50° F demarcation line, get out there and open your hive for a quick check. Make sure to gear up and smoke the hive just like you did in the spring, summer and fall. The bees may be a bit cranky from the cold. Peer down between the frames. Does the hive look healthy? Are there an abnormal number of dead bees at the bottom? Pull out a couple of the frames and look for food stores. Does the colony have four or five frames with plenty of capped honey? If not, you may consider starting to feed them. If you do begin feeding your colony, you must continue feeding them until the first nectar flows. You will know it is flowing when you see bees coming back to the hive with pollen in the baskets. Try and limit this late winter check to just a few minutes. Close up the hive and make any notes in your hive notebook. If you need to feed them, get on it right away. If not, come back and check again in a couple weeks on a nice sunny day.

Second, go back through your hive notebook. Are there things you would like to change for your hive this year? Would you like to move them to a better location? If you didn't have them on a hive stand, would you like them on one this year? If everything was great last year, you most likely don't need to make any changes. But it helps to go through the hive notebook just to make sure you haven't forgotten any important details. It will also help you plan out your activities for the upcoming year.

One thing nice about a bee colony is you can make two from one. If you are judicious about when you do this, you can double the number of colonies you have with minimal expense other than the extra hive parts and the cost of a queen. A split is beneficial to prevent a strong and booming colony from swarming. The very best time to split a hive is in the early spring, just a few weeks before the flowers start to bloom. In my area, this means early April.

To split or divide a colony there are just a few easy steps.

First, set up your new hive with all the parts in place.

Second, purchase a new queen. You can normally do this through the same place you purchased your first colony. Most places will have queens in stock ready to be purchased. If you need to order her through the mail, do this.

Third, once your queen arrives, or the day before if you prefer, open up your new hive. Take off the upper hive body box. Remove four frames from the middle of the lower brood box, if you are splitting your hive from just one source colony. You can actually take frames, larvae, and brood bees from several hives if you want to make one colony from two or three. If you are going this route, take out five to seven of the middle frames.

Fourth, open the source hive. Make sure you smoke it properly. Pull out several frames with brood bees, capped larvae, and capped honey. Check each one very carefully to make sure you aren't removing the queen from the hive. This is critical; don't take the queen from the source colony. Then, place the frame with the bees and brood from the source hive into the new hive. Do this with four frames if you are splitting from just one hive. If you are splitting from two take three from each. If you are splitting from three, take two or three from each. Replace the empty frame slot with a frame from your new hive.

Note: If you are pulling from several source hives, don't open them all up at the same time. Open one, finish with it and close it up before you open your second hive.

Now, your new colony should have several frames full of foundation, larvae, and brood bees. The bees from different colonies won't fight because none of them are on their "home turf". If you are going to introduce the new queen into her colony right away just follow the steps you took when you first hived a colony. Place the queen cage hanging from one of the middle frames with a candy plug in the hole. Check in a couple days to make sure she is out. If she is, you just made one colony into two. Congratulations.

This colony must be fed until the nectar flows. It may even do better than your first colony since it has the advantage of worker bees, larvae, and several frames with wax comb already built up. As a precaution, you may want to feed the colonies you took frames out of as well. This will ensure their quick "recuperation".

Sometimes, when you have a few weak colonies going into

the winter months, it makes more sense to combine two colonies into one hive rather than have two that may not make it through the lean months. Or, if you have just one weak colony and one strong one, you can combine them into an extra strong colony, thereby saving resources and reducing the chance one may die off.

The process may sound dangerous to the bees. Won't they fight? Actually, if done right, they will merge without a complaint. Here is what you do:

First, figure out which colony is the strongest. This will be your new home base.

Second, smoke the weaker colony and open it up. Go through each frame carefully in both the hive body boxes. Reduce the hive to just one box with the ten best frames. While you are doing this, if you see the queen, kill her. If you haven't found her, you can just go ahead with the process if you are the gambling type. I prefer not to. I find the queen and dispose of her. If you leave both queens alive going into this process, there is a chance the weaker queen may kill the stronger queen. They will fight and one will win. If the weak queen lives, this would leave you with a weak colony that just doesn't realize it yet. I suggest you go into the process with just the stronger hive being queenright.

Now, smoke the stronger hive. Lift the top off the hive. Place two or three layers of newspaper on top of the upper hive box. Place the inner and outer tops back on the hive. You now have one really strong hive with three deep hive boxes. Wait a few days. If everything goes right, the bees will slowly chew holes in the newspaper and begin to mingle. By the time they get through, their scents will be so intermingled they will feel as if they are just one big happy family.

If they haven't chewed through in two or three days, slide your hive tool through the newspaper in several spots. Then close the hive up and wait a few more days. Next time you check, they should be nicely mixed together.

If all is right, open up the hive and reduce the three boxes down to two. Move brood frames down with the other brood frames and pick just the best frames to keep. Once you are done, you should have one box with the ten "weakest" frames in it to use with your now empty hive. Next year you can put a new colony in it. Or, if another of your colonies is really strong, you could split that colony and fill up your now empty hive immediately.

Diseases, Pests and Other Problems

Diseases

Let us now speak of diseases. For the most part, if you properly medicate your bees, you will probably never see any of these diseases. There is always a chance. So it is best you are prepared for them and can properly identify any situations which may develop. Each time you open up your hive you should look for signs of disease. If you see any, investigate carefully and take care of your bees.

What diseases can affect your bees?   In alphabetical order they are:

1.   American foulbrood

2.   Chalkbrood

3.   Chilled Brood

4.   Dysentery

5.   European foulbrood

6.   Nosema

7.   Sacbrood

8.   Stonebrood

Just reading this list makes it seem disaster is lurking around the corner. Take heart, most of these diseases are just something you will read about. Let's talk about the symptoms so you can identify if your bees do happen to come down with something. We will also discuss what you should do to best help your hive if they get one of these diseases. I am going to address the foulbroods first and then stonebrood, sacbrood and chilled brood. These are health issues that affect the larvae. Then I will go through nosema, dysentery and paralysis which are diseases which affect the adult bees.

American Foulbrood

American foulbrood not only is the first disease on our list, it is most definitely the worst. Sometimes called AFB, it is caused by bacteria. This disease kills capped brood. What you will see in your hive are dark brown larvae. The caps begin to sink and sag. The caps may even look like they have tiny holes in them. Another issue is the brood begins to be spotty across the frame. Instead of an occasional unfilled cell, you may see many that are unused. The tops of the caps will most likely also look greasy or slick with moisture. There will likely be a sour smell emanating from the hive.

If you see these symptoms, go wash your hands very carefully. This isn't communicable to humans, but you don't want to get it on your equipment. Any equipment that may have touched it must be left there—under no circumstances should you use that equipment on any other hive.

Get a toothpick or small stick and stick it into one of the infected brood cells. Stir it around and then slowly withdraw it from the cell. If you have American foulbrood, the brood will stretch out—sometimes referred to as roping out—and will then snap back into the cell. It will stretch a bit like candy taffy and then it will spring back like a released rubber band.

If you have a case of American foulbrood, most, if not all

states require you to call the state bee inspector responsible for apiary concerns in your area. In most cases, if they confirm your suspicions, they will have you burn your hive and equipment. This seems to be the safest way to ensure the disease doesn't spread. My advice is even if your state doesn't require it, call in an expert and after they check your hive, burn it immediately. It isn't fair to other beekeepers to treat this without the urgency it requires. The only guaranteed cure is to destroy the hive.

To adequately kill the hive, you will need to burn all the bees so the bacteria cannot spread. You will also need to actually burn all the boxes and frames as well. Although many people feel that if you char the entire box and the tops with a blowtorch it is enough to stop any future colonies from getting sick, I feel it is safer to just burn all the parts of the infected hive. The purchase of new hive boxes and frames more than makes up for the possibility of spreading the disease to all my other hives as well as other beekeeper's hives. It is up to you which method you take. Don't ever keep the frames, just burn them. But please, make sure you do something adequate so you don't get the rest of your hives sick or any other beekeeper's hives sick.

For this reason, if you ever choose to buy used equipment from a beekeeper, make sure you know enough to ask them if their hive died and if so, what caused it. You should also carefully sanitize any equipment you do buy on the used market.

European Foulbrood

Next we have European foulbrood. Also known as EFB, this disease is also a bacterial disease that affects the larvae. With EFB, the bacterium actually kills the larvae before they are capped instead of after they are capped like with AFB. You will notice that many of the larvae are dead in their cells and are uncapped. If any are capped, they too will be sunken but when you stick a toothpick into the cell it won't pull out a stringy or ropy trail. The larvae that are uncapped will look twisted in their cell like tiny corkscrews and will most likely be a light tan or brownish color. The entire hive may smell a bit sour.

The EFB bacterium attacks the middle gut of the larva which

causes them to contort and twist in their cells before they are capped. The frames may smell slightly fishy, and all ages of larvae will show symptoms. Often this disease presents in early spring.

The best prevention is regular application of Terramycin. It is incredibly inexpensive and should probably just be administered on a regular basis even though EFB isn't that common in the US. To prepare, just mix the recommended dose with some powdered sugar and just set it on a piece of paper on top of the frames. The medicine, if it shakes down onto brood, is too strong for them at this stage. That is the reason for setting it on a piece of paper. Administer Terramycin three times five days apart both in the spring and in the fall. In the spring, give it to your bees about a month before you put the supers on your hive. In the fall, give it to your bees after the harvest.

If you do get EFB in your hive, destroy the colony right away. Then thoroughly sanitize the box and all the frames. I would put new wax foundation in my frames. And then, when you put a new colony in the hive, make sure to administer Terramycin regularly. With these steps, you shouldn't have a repeat of EFB.

Chalkbrood

Chalkbrood comes from a fungus. Most often found in spring when there are moist and damp conditions, it is a reasonably common affliction. You will know it when you see larvae that are a chalky white color. The larvae will also become hard, almost like a small piece of chalk. Some of the dead larvae may be black instead of white. If you see chalky dead larvae outside your hive, you have chalkbrood.

There is no medicine to resolve the problem. It will generally resolve itself as conditions warm up and the area becomes less wet and damp. The only thing you can do is monitor the hive and help clean up any carcasses left near the hive. You can get into your hive and look at each of the frames. If one or two of the frames seem to have an excessive number of dead chalkbrood affected larvae, you can remove the frame and replace it with a new one. This will help the hive "get ahead" of the disease and reduce the workload of those responsible for removing the affected larvae. If you do this, disinfect the removed frames and replace the wax foundation.

Because chalkbrood is caused by wet and damp conditions, look at where your hive is positioned. Can you get it into another area where conditions won't be so wet in the spring? An easy fix is to put it on a stand. By lifting the hive up a bit, you will reduce the amount of moisture that gets into the hive.

Stonebrood

Stonebrood is another fungal disease. It causes the brood to become mummified. The dead brood will become black and very hard. When first infected, the individual larva gets the fungus spores in their gut and it eventually erupts through the skin of the larva. When worker bees come along to care for and clean the larva, they carry the spores and can infect other brood. For the most part, there is not much you can do to assist or help the hive. The best thing to do is allow the colony to remove the mummies and hopefully the colony will recover. Sometimes they will not. If you do notice a buildup of mummies near the entrance of the hive, put on a pair of rubber gloves and dispose of the mummies. It will help the colony keep clean and defeat the fungus. This is an extremely rare disease and is not often seen.

Sacbrood

Sacbrood needs to be discussed next. Caused by a virus, this is not a serious threat to your colony. The larvae that get it will be a bit yellowish turning to dark brown. The comb may appear a bit like EFB or AFB affected comb. It will be spotty with several of the caps chewed and torn. The difference is the dead larvae don't disintegrate as they do with both AFB and EFB into a nasty mess. Instead, the dead larvae will be found on the bottom of the cell with a leathery feel to them. They will also have what seems to be a water filled sac. Hence the name.

There is no known cure for sacbrood. Like any virus, it will run its course and after the bees build up enough immunity to the virus, they will recover. You can help by cleaning out the dead if you would like, but otherwise this is one that just will go away on its own. If it doesn't go away, one solution that may help is to requeen the colony. The new queen will most likely not have the same genetic susceptibility to the sacbrood virus and with the new royal; the colony will be able to get on with its life.

Chilled Brood

Chilled brood is the most common issue to affect larvae and of least concern to the overall health of the hive. It mostly hits in the time between late winter and early spring; especially in areas where the weather changes back and forth between cold and somewhat warm days. During a run of warmer weather the queen can get nature's signal to start rearing brood in an effort to grow the colony to spring and summer levels. This is the time of year when the colony is at its smallest. The weather then changes back to cold and the colony goes back into a cluster. The cluster will form around the queen. The cluster will also try and keep the brood warm, but sometimes the size of the colony cluster is too small and some of the newly laid brood is left out in the cold. The brood left outside the cluster dies. If you are checking your hive in early spring and see a circular ring of dead brood that doesn't seem sick or diseased, this is most likely what happened. It isn't anything to worry about, nor is there anything you can do to prevent it. The bees will clean out the carcasses and life in the hive will go on. I bring up chilled brood merely to make you aware of what you are seeing if you see a ring of dead larvae on one of your frames.

On to diseases that affect the adult bees. Although these aren't as serious as the previously discussed afflictions, they can slow the production of the hive significantly and reduce your honey harvest.

Nosema

The most common is nosema. Caused by the *Nosema apis* single cell protozoan, this disease affects the intestinal tract of adult bees. If you see several bees outside of the hive crawling around seemingly lost, bees that are twitching or shivering, or bees that seem to have their wings bent at strange angles it is possible the colony has nosema.

Remember I said that bees are meticulously clean. They never relieve themselves in the hive, going to such extremes in the winter as to gain 50% of their body weight in waste they are holding in until they can get out of the hive on a warm day and relive themselves. Well, nosema destroys their best intentions. If you see streaks of fecal matter throughout the hive and in the entrance areas, your colony most likely has nosema.

A side effect of Nosema is that it actually prevents young bees from developing the glands that produce royal jelly. This makes them unable to properly take care of brood. A queen with nosema will have a precipitous drop in egg laying and may quit completely. This means the hive must supersede her and the lost time can set a hive back so severely that it may not recover and produce any significant amounts of honey for the year. For this reason alone, the small expense of the medicine that will help prevent it is well worth the investment.

To prevent nosema, you can administer Fumidil B to your hive in the fall. Fumidil B is mixed with a sugar syrup feeding. The next best prevention for Nosema is your hive location. Make sure your hive is not in a cold and wet location, that it has plenty of good airflow, and the colony has access to clean water.

If your hive does have nosema, there isn't much you can do except make sure the hive is positioned in the best possible location for optimal health. Make sure they are in a dry area with minimal wind. And then, make sure you administer Fumidil B to all your bees in the fall. Your hive will most likely survive; it will just lose some time, possibly even the entire season. In this regard, nosema is a bit like the flu in humans, once you have it, there isn't much you can do except get as comfortable as possible and wait it out.

Paralysis

Paralysis, the next issue on our list, comes from various bee viruses. The most common symptoms are abnormal shaking and trembling of the wings and body. You may see the bees crawling around the front of the hive. There can sometimes be more than a thousand bees affected from a single colony. The bees may have bloated abdomens and their wings will look somewhat open or bent at strange angles. The affected bees may be prevented from entering the hive by the guards. Death for the afflicted follows soon after.

There is no known cure for the various paralysis viruses. The best thing you can do is watch the hive. If the problems continue, you should requeen your hive. It seems that genetics play a large role in the bee's susceptibility to the virus. By introducing a new blood line into the colony, you most likely will solve the issue of the virus causing paralysis.

Dysentery

Dysentery comes mostly from long periods of time stuck in

the hive due to cold weather. The bees become too full of feces and begin to void in the hive. If too many of the bees do this, the hive will become streaked with feces and disease will spread. It can actually kill the colony or drive them to swarm in search of a cleaner location. Dry, warm weather is the real cure to dysentery.

The next best solution for dysentery is to keep an eye on the weather. If there is typically a period of three weeks or more of below 50° F, you may want to consider keeping your hives in a ventilated building during the cold times.

If you notice a colony seems to have lots of feces streaking inside or outside the hive, you can help them get better by feeding dry sugar or a very heavy 2:1 syrup mixture. The dry food reduces the amount of moisture in the bee's gut and can assist in preventing and curing an attack of dysentery.

Pests

Pests that attack your hive range in size from the tiny mite all the way up to bears. Let's discuss the various pests and how to best protect your hive from them. Just like with the diseases that can affect your precious bees, the goal of this chapter is to enable you to identify the pests that may be affecting your hive. If you can identify the pest, then you can take steps to remedy the problem.

Parasitic mites can be the most devastating of all pests to your bee colony. Varroa mites and tracheal mites are the two most commonly found mites in a bee colony.

Tracheal Mites

Tracheal mites, also known as the *Acarapis woodi*, are found, as you probably already suspected, in the trachea of the bee. Because they are so small and live inside the bee, you aren't going to see them in the hive, instead, you are looking for the effects of tracheal mites on your colony. When infected with these mites, individual bees have their trachea perforated and live shorter lives. With a mass infection in the colony, the colony can be weakened enough to destroy it.

There are a few signs that your colony may have an infestation of these pesky critters. Many of the symptoms are the same or similar to a colony with nosema. If you see any of these symptoms, first rule out nosema—it is more likely the cause than mites.

If your colony has many bees walking around the front of the hive like they are disoriented or drunk, it could be tracheal mites. You may also see bees attempting to climb and then launch into flight but falling before they are able to fly. Both of these are caused by a lack of oxygen. As the trachea is perforated, the bees get less and less oxygen, eventually dying. You may also notice bees with strangely angled wings. All three of these issues will also be seen in a nosema infection, so, as I said rule out nosema first. If you are sure it isn't nosema, then it may be tracheal mites. If so, you can treat with menthol crystals.

Menthol crystals don't have a perfect record of curing the

issue, but they are the only known remedy that can possibly solve the infestation. Purchase menthol crystals from your beekeeping supplier and place them in the back of the hive. They come in a little mesh bag. Leave them in the bag and treat your hive for at least two weeks.

A few studies have shown menthol is most effective between 60° F and 80° F. If the temperature is on the lower end of that range, place the crystals on top of a piece of tinfoil inside the hive and set the tinfoil on top of your brood boxes. If the temperature is closer to the high end, place the menthol on tinfoil inside the hive down on the bottom board of your hive.

If you are treating your bees with any medications, you must remove any upper supers from your hive before you begin treating the colony. Remember, any time you medicate, remove the supers. You don't want that medication to get into honey you are going to consume or sell for consumption. It just isn't healthy.

Some people feel that feeding their bees grease patties helps control tracheal mites. I have never tried it, but it may be something interesting for you to try. Just mix up 1 cup of shortening with 3 cups of sugar and 3 TBS of honey. Mix it up into several patties about the size of a hamburger. Place one in your hive on top of some waxed paper on top of the upper hive body frames. Store the rest in your freezer for later. Every week or so, pull open the top of your hive. If the previous patty is gone or mostly gone, put another in the hive.

The young bees will eat the grease patties and the scent of the grease will keep the tracheal mites from viewing them as a potential food source. So the older, infected bees will still die, but the young bees avoid getting infected and will live. Treat this way for four to six weeks, thereby giving all the new young a chance to grow up without being infected. Grease patties are also an easy way to feed the hive in a pinch. Keep a few in your freezer for an extended cold snap and you will have a ready food source that may get a threatened hive through the toughest part of the winter.

Varroa Mites

A varroa mite infection is easier to identify. Officially

known as the *Varroa destructor mite,* these pests are parasites which actually ride on the back of your honeybees. If you see a roundish looking black spot on the body of your bees, you probably have a varroa infestation. Under a microscope, the varroa mites look like tiny crabs. A varroa infestation can cause several latent viruses naturally found in the hive to proliferate and destroy the hive.

A screened bottom board will help the hive combat an infestation. As the mites fall off bees, they fall through the screen and are unable to climb back up for another attack.

The very best treatment for the varroa mite is Apistan® or one of other products designed to kill the varroa mite such as Apiguard®, CheckMite+® or formic acid. I use Apistan® just because I was introduced to it first and am comfortable with it. It comes in long, thick strips somewhat similar to fly paper. You hang these strips in the hive between the 3rd and 4th frames and the 7th and 8th frames. The bees walk on them and are medicated as they come in contact with the strips. The strips should be left in the hive for between six and eight weeks. Most beekeepers use strips in the spring and fall. Remember, when medicating, make sure there are no upper supers on your hive. You don't want your food to be medicated.

Wax Moth

Next up in our lineup of pests is the wax moth. *Galleria mellonella L* will wreak havoc on your unoccupied frames or weak hives. This moth lays its eggs in the fall and the tiny moth larvae crawl into the hive and burrow into the small cracks and crevices. As they grow, they chew through the wax honeycomb and leave a nasty mess of cocoons and webbing. An active, strong hive will have no problem with these little critters. Cold kills the moth in all stages of life, but, if you live in an area where there is no extended frost, they will absolutely demolish your stored boxes and frames. There is no approved method to kill the moth off except cold. The easiest method to control them in warm areas is to put your frames in a deep freezer for a few days. This will kill any adults and all the eggs and larvae. Then you should be able to wrap your stored boxes up so they are ready for the next year. Commercial beekeepers use a carbon dioxide room to suffocate the wax moths, but that is much too expensive for the backyard beekeeper.

Rodents, Birds and More

Mice and other rodents are another nuisance that can cause issues for your hive. In the fall, mice look to your hives as a somewhat protected area from the vagaries of winter. To keep the mice out, first check your hives. If you see mice droppings, you have an issue. If you don't see droppings, you most likely don't have a problem. If you think you have a problem, check your hive to make sure no mice are in it and then put a mouse guard across the entrance of the hive. A mouse guard is a metal guard with holes small enough for the bees to fly through during the winter months but much too small for a mouse to get in.

Some birds will wait outside your hive to eat the bees as they come and go. If you notice a serious problem, you need to take action. Most birds won't eat enough bees to make a difference but a jay might destroy an entire hive with time. And a few other birds may do the same. Simplest, if you live in an area where it is practicable and legal, is to shoot the marauders. If this solution doesn't appeal to you, work on some type of scarecrow, metal wind chime or other item to scare off the birds.

Skunks will come around and scratch and dig at your hive. As the bees come out to see what the ruckus is, the skunks will eat them up. Think honey candy wrapped in a tiny protein package. The little bees taste like sweet treats to the skunk. Once skunks have their eye on your hive, you need to do whatever necessary to get rid of them. The easiest solution to prevent a skunk attack is to put your hive up on a stand.

Raccoons are a different story. These intelligent invaders will just climb right up a stand. They can even get your beehive open if given enough time. The best solution I have ever seen for a raccoon invasion is a modified latch to keep the lid locked closed. The cheapest solution is a large rock on top of the beehive. The weight will generally deter the raccoon from getting in.

Bears love honey. They will absolutely destroy your hive. If you live in an area where bears exist, the only permanent deterrent is an electric fence.

Fun Beetivities

Balms and Salves

Lip Balm

Homemade beeswax lip balm is simple and easy to make. It will only take you about 15 minutes and the resulting lip balm will keep your entire family's lips perfect through the entire winter season. Here is what you need to fill about 15-20 lip balm tubes or 10 .25 ounce jars. If you want to make a bigger batch, just double it or triple it.

- Containers. I use small 1/4 ounce jars but you can use lip balm tubes or tins. Whatever floats your boat.
- 2 Tablespoons Beeswax
- 4 Tablespoons Coconut Oil
- Vitamin E gel capsules (1 or 2 is plenty)
- Essential Oil such as anise (supposedly an aphrodisiac), peppermint or eucalyptus. Essential oils aren't necessary, but can add a nice touch to your lip balm.

How do the ingredients work? The beeswax is an emollient. It helps keep your lips moist and supple by creating a barrier between them and the harsh winter air. The vitamin E oil will prolong the shelf life of your lip balm. The coconut oil is antibacterial and moisturizing, both of which will help your lips. The fatty acids in the coconut oil also create a barrier that locks in moisture, reducing the chance of your lips cracking. Essential oils add flavors, smells and possibly some health benefits to your lip balm.

Now here are the steps to make this fantastic lip balm. If you have a double boiler, use that. If not, put a small pot of water on the stove and stick a canning jar in the water. Make sure no water gets in the jar. Turn the stove on medium heat. When the water is warm, put all the ingredients, except the vitamin E and the essential oil, in the double boiler or jar. Let them slowly melt. Once they are fully melted, stir them gently. To test, put a small bit on a spoon and put the spoon in the fridge for five or ten minutes. Test the bit on the spoon. If you feel your lip balm mix is too hard, add a bit more oil to the mixture. If it is too soft, add a bit more beeswax. Now turn off the heat. Stir in the essential oil and the vitamin E. Now transfer the liquid into your containers. This is why I prefer jars—because I think they are easier to fill. Use a small funnel if necessary. Let the tubes, jars or tins cool. Put the lids on. Label and use, share or sell them.

Salves

There are many herbs which are good for healing. Some of the most powerful herbs you can use for healing and soothing itches caused by rashes or insect bites are plantain, comfrey and chickweed. You can make this simple crock pot salve without the chickweed or echinacea if necessary, but it is best if you can get all the items.

Here are the ingredients you will need.

- 1/2 cup fresh plantain
- 1/2 cup fresh chickweed

- 1/2 cup fresh echinacea

- 1/4 cup fresh comfrey

- 2 1/2 cups olive oil

- 1/8 cup of beeswax

- Vitamin E gel caps (I use three for this recipe)

Now that you have everything ready, wash and dry your herbs. Wait until they just are starting to wilt on your counter. Place your herbs in your crock pot. Pour the olive oil on top of them. You need the herbs to be fully covered by the oil, so you may need to add more oil depending on the shape of your crock pot.

Turn the heat on low and let the herbs sit for about 4 hours. Turn the heat off and let the oil cool. When cool enough to work with, pour the oil through a cheesecloth strainer to get out all the herbs. I sometimes just use an old cloth or t shirt. Squeeze out the excess oil.

Now, put the oil back in your empty crock pot. Add the beeswax. When fully melted take a bit of the mixture in a teaspoon and stick it in the fridge. After three or four minutes, pull the spoon out. The bit on the spoon will be the consistency of your salve when it is done. If you want it to be softer, add more oil. If you want it to be harder, add more beeswax.

When it is just right, turn off the heat and add the vitamin E. I just nip the end off the gel caps and squeeze it into the mixture. Stir it briefly. Pour it into containers. I like to put it into 1 ounce jars, but you can put it in whatever you like. Label it. Use it, share it, or sell it. You will be amazed at how fast this salve heals an assortment of cuts, burns and rashes. Once again, I am not a doctor and do not claim to be one. I just really like my salve.

Let There Be Light: Making Candles

Dipped Candles

To make hand dipped candles with beeswax is an easy process. Beeswax is often preferred for dipped tapers because the beeswax burns slow making for a long lasting candle. Plus the layers of wax go on fairly thick, making them quick and easy to produce.

The ingredients you will need are some beeswax, some square braid wick (#2/0 is great) and a deep double boiler. If you don't have a double boiler, just put some water in a stock pot on your stove and stick a quart jar in the water.

To make these beautiful tapers put your double boiler on the stove and turn to medium heat. You will want the wax to be around 165° F, so adjust the stove temperature so the water is about 170° F. When the water is the right temperature, put your unmelted wax in the deep double boiler to melt.

Once the wax is fully melted, cut a length of wick that is

twice the length of your intended candle plus 2". For instance, if you want a 10" taper, cut the wick to 22". Your tapers can't be produced taller than the depth of your double boiler. If you want taller tapers, you need a deeper double boiler.

Now cut a small piece of wire to hold your wick from the top while you are dipping it. Tie weights such as a pair of nuts (the kind that attach to a bolt) to each end of the string. These will pull the wick straight to the bottom of the melted wax.

Dip your tapers into the wax slowly and then pull them out slowly. The first time they won't accumulate much wax on them. Hold them or hang them for a couple of minutes so the wax has time to harden just a bit. If you don't wait long enough between dips, the wax will fall off the wick and you will have to start the process over.

Dip them again and again until they are the desired thickness. As you dip the candles, try and make the dip and the removal one smooth, continuous movement. Dip slowly to the bottom, as soon as they reach the bottom, begin to pull them slowly out. If you stop, you will begin to "lose" more wax than you are gaining while it is in the melted wax.

After three or four dips, while the tapers are waiting for their next dip, cut off the weights from the bottom of each taper. Dip three, four or even more times until your beeswax tapers are just how you want them. Now, hang them to dry for a day or two.

For storage purposes, it is best to hang them until they are ready to use. When you are ready, snip the wick between the two tapers and voila, you have two beautiful beeswax candles ready for your next romantic dinner. Or you can use them to light the house if the power goes out. Romance, self reliance, and preparedness all in one great candle.

Poured Candles

Beeswax candles have a classic golden glow and a delicious hint of honey scent. As an alternative to paraffin based candles, handmade beeswax candles not only look and smell better, they are actually healthier for you. Paraffin based candles release toxins into the air. Beeswax, when burned, produces negative ions that attach to positively charged particles such as pollen, dust and other pollutants in the air. These newly bound, neutralized ions fall down to the ground. So if you suffer from hay fever or allergies, burning beeswax candles can actually help clean the air you breathe.

To make a simple poured candle all you need is some beeswax, a candle container, a wick and some time. Here is what I use to make my candles.

- 2 pounds of filtered beeswax
- 1 cup of coconut oil
- 18-24 inches of cotton wick
- Scissors to cut wick
- 10-12 popsicle sticks, straws or pencils
- 10 -- 8 oz Ball Mason Jars, or if you want larger candles you can use six 12 oz jars or four wide mouth pint jars
- Double boiler or crock pot
- Thermometer
- Essential Oil of your choice (optional)

Set out your jars. Start to melt your wax in the double boiler or crock pot. You don't want the wax to get over 160° F. The melting point of beeswax is about 147° F, so if you can keep the temperature closer to 150° F it is even better.

While you are waiting for the wax to melt , cut a wick for each jar so that the wick touches the bottom of the jar and extends above the jar about two inches. Tie each wick around the stick, pencil or straw that you are using and hang them down into the jar. The end of the wick should just touch the bottom of the jar.

Now, back to your beeswax. When your beeswax is fully melted, add the coconut oil. At this time, you can also add any essential oils you may want to use for your candle. I especially like star anise or lemongrass. Just add 15 to 25 drops.

Now, with your jars all set up with wicks in them, begin to pour just a bit of the wax down into the jar. Try to pour the wax so it coats the wick on the way to the bottom of the jar. As soon as you have a small pool of wax in the bottom of the jar and coating the wick, stop pouring. Pouring wax along the wick will help ensure your wick is straight. Let it harden just enough so that the wick is held by the wax in the bottom of the jar.

Once your wick is set in place, slowly pour enough wax into the jar to fill it to where you think it looks perfect. Pour gently so you don't knock the wick off center. Let the candle set for a couple of days. Trim the wick so only about ¼" to ½" shows above the candle.

Light and enjoy.

Recipes

Honey Wheat Bread

Several years ago, I was looking around for a great wheat bread recipe. I got my mom's favorite recipe and my mother in law's favorite recipe and made them both. They were both fantastic. As I sat looking at the two recipes, I realized there were many similarities and a few differences. I decided to blend the two into one. What I ended up with is one of the best homemade wheat bread recipes I have ever found. I'm convinced a big part of it is the home grown honey and the freshly ground flour. You can actually make it with white flour if you prefer, but I think the fresh wheat flour is so much better. In fact, I humbly like to call it the World's Best Homemade Wheat Bread.

Here is the ingredient list to make a two loaf batch. You can easily double it or even half it for a larger or smaller batch.

- 7 Cups Wheat Flour

- 2 3/4 Cups Water

- 1/8 Cup Oil

- 1 TBS salt

- 1 1/2 TBS yeast

- 1 TBS dough enhancer

- 1/3 Cup honey

- 1/4 Cup molasses

- 1/8 Cup lecithin

- 1 TBS gluten

Here are the steps to make the bread. First, grind the wheat in your wheat grinder. I prefer a half and half blend of hard white and hard red winter wheat. More white wheat makes fluffier bread and more red makes more dense bread. Put half of the newly ground flour in the mixer. Then add the water and mix it on medium speed for two minutes with a dough hook. Add the oil (I use olive oil but vegetable oil works as well), salt, yeast, dough enhancer, honey, molasses, lecithin and gluten. Now mix it on high for another two minutes. Now turn the mixer down to low and begin adding the flour. Add one cup first and then half a cup every minute or so.

Keep adding flour until the dough pulls off the mixer walls. Be careful—if you add too much flour, you will end up with nasty dry loaves of bread. Sometimes, if I want really fluffy bread, I substitute a cup of white flour for a cup of the wheat flour—but mostly I don't. Once your dough is pulled off the bowl walls mix it for about a minute or two. Now, pull out your bread pans. I just use glass or metal 9x5 loaf pans, but you can use any size you prefer. Spray the pans with PAM or wipe them down with a pat of butter. Now pull the dough out and divide it in two parts. Carefully fold the dough balls by pulling the sides out and folding them under the loaf. Try and get a longish piece that fits in your pan nicely. Now do the other. Put the pans in a COLD oven to rise.

Let the loaves rise for 30 to 60 minutes. After the dough has risen to the top edge of the pan (if you use all hard red wheat they sometimes don't rise quite this much so just wait an hour), turn the oven on to 350° F and cook the loaves for 30 to 35 minutes. I live at 4500 feet above sea level so adjust accordingly to where you live and what size pans you are using. Once your bread is nice and golden on top, pull it out of the oven and set it on a rack to cool. Wait 5 seconds and then cut yourself a nice fat slice and eat it. It tastes even better if you slather it with honey. I would say wait longer than 5 seconds, but in my house we are lucky to wait even 5 seconds. The first loaf is normally gone within a few minutes.

Fruit Leather

Making fruit leather is fun and simple. This recipe is designed for apricot fruit leather, but nearly any fruit can be substituted. Blend raw fruit until you have seven cups of pureed fruit. Pour it into a saucepan. Add one cup honey. Put it on low heat and stir occasionally until it just begins to simmer. Once it simmers, pour it onto dehydrator trays and dehydrate until it is ready. You will know it is ready when the fruit leather pulls out of the trays in one piece, but isn't tough. In my dehydrator it takes about 12 hours. It helps if you pour equal amounts into each tray, that way all the trays get finished at the same time.

Once it is ready, pull it off the trays. Cut into serving size pieces with a pair of scissors. Wrap with saran wrap and store it in an airtight container or freeze it for later. To wrap it, just lay a piece of saran wrap on your counter that is slightly larger than the piece of fruit leather you are going to wrap. Lay the fruit leather on top of the saran wrap, centered. Roll it up. Voila, healthy treats for the whole family. This past summer, we harvested several thousand apricots from our tree. It was a bumper crop. Most of it ended up as fruit leather. We love it so much; the apricot fruit leather was disappearing faster than we could produce it. And you know it has none of the ridiculous preservatives you get from store bought products. Just fruit, honey and a bit of time and love.

Honey Lemon Tea

Honey lemon tea is another favorite in our house. My wife starts every day with a cup of honey lemon tea. Simply heat up seven ounces of water to the temperature you prefer. Add the juice from a 1/4 of a lemon. Add one heaping tablespoon of honey and stir it up. This is a great way to get your daily dose of honey. My kids like it with a dash of cinnamon also.

It tastes great and the combination of honey and lemon helps ward off many nasty illnesses. In fact, here is a short list of things honey can do for your health:

1. It is anti-bacterial and anti-fungal and helps ward off bacterial and fungal infections. Specifically, it has been shown to retard the growth of E.coli and salmonella. It has also been shown to be effective against some *Staphylococcus aureus* infections.

2. Reduces ulcers and other gastrointestinal disorders

3. Contains antioxidants that can reduce heart disease

4. Reduces coughs and throat irritations. It has been shown in a few studies to be more effective than common cough medicines that contain dextromethorphan.

5. Used for wound care—keeps wounds from festering and helps them heal properly. Because it is hydroscopic, it pulls moisture out of wounds. It is also antiseptic and anti bacterial which means it helps keep wounds free from infection.

6. Some lab studies have suggested that honey helps

ease pollen allergies. Most experts believe that the tiny bit of pollen contained in all honey helps inoculate people against allergies. This seems to only work with local honey that hasn't been pasteurized. The local honey contains pollens that affect the allergic individual as opposed to honey from other areas, which wouldn't contain the correct pollen particulates to properly inoculate the individual.

7. Some studies suggest it may help fight GERD (Gastroesophageal reflux).

Although I am not a doctor, there have been several studies which show these health benefits to be true. In my mind, a daily dose of honey definitely can't hurt, and it may just make all the difference.

Final Words

There are many joys to be found in beekeeping. The greatest joy comes from working hand in hand with bees to achieve greater self-sufficiency for you and your family. Working with your family and friends, you can build a reliable and steady source of nutrition right in your own backyard. After you get your first hive, I'm quite certain you will enjoy it so much, you will decide to get another, and then another. Who knows where it will end for you?

Many people ask me; do you make money with bees? You most certainly can. It is estimated that over 200,000 people keep bees in the United States alone. Some are just hobbyists that make little or no money with their bees, but they get honey for themselves and perhaps a few friends. Next are sideline beekeepers. These are serious part time beekeepers with up to 300 hives. Finally there are commercial beekeepers. Some of them have up to 80,000 hives. No matter where you want to end up, you can get there with a bit of effort. Even the biggest commercial operations started out just where you are today, with an interest in beekeeping and one hive.

For most people, the joy of having a self sufficient source of honey is enough and they will want just one, two or a few hives.

Others will want to go big and make a career out of beekeeping. Whichever route you decide, it is best to start small and work your way into it. Buy a hive or two and practice for a year before you decide to go all in as a beekeeper. That way, at the end of a year, you will have a good idea of what it takes and if you enjoy it enough to do it full time.

Thanks for reading this book. As with any project, there are countless people who have assisted me in this endeavor. The biggest thanks go to Camylle for everything. She patiently puts up with my frequent and varied obsessions as well as my insistence on going all in on every new project. Thanks also to my wonderful children who have patiently watched me and my obsession with bees, even when the bees interfere with their desire to run barefoot through the grass. Also thanks to all my friends and family who not only have encouraged me and shared in my joy and love of beekeeping, they have also been patient with me as I drone on (pun intended) about bees and how wonderful they are. A special thanks to Dave for working side by side with me on our hives.

If you have any comments or suggestions, feel free to share them with me at my website, www.urbanhomesteadbooks.com.

Also, as you most likely know, an author's lifeblood is a good review. If you enjoyed this book, please spend a moment and leave a comment on Amazon where it is sold. Other people rely heavily on reader's comments there and your kind words can make a world of difference.

May the greatest joys of beekeeping be yours as you embark on this great adventure.

Trevor

<u>Glossary</u>

Africanized honey bee: A highly aggressive bee species that resulted from a cross of bees from Africa and Brazil. Sometimes referred to as the "killer bee".

Apiary: What is colloquially known as the beeyard. This is any place you keep a hive.

Apiculture: The science and study of beekeeping.

Apis mellifera: The official scientific name for the European honey bee.

Bee bread: Pollen after it has been collected by bees and mixed with honey and other substances. This is then stored in the comb to be used for larvae and bee food. High in protein.

Bee Brush: A brush used to sweep the bees clear of frames.

Bee Space: The distance between comb that varies between a quarter of an inch and half an inch. This space will not be filled by the bees and is used as passageways through the hive.

Beehive: Any space used by the bees to live. A colony resides in a beehive, whether it is a rock crevice, an attic, or the boxes in your apiary.

Beeswax: A substance created by the worker bees that is used to build comb. Once harvested by a beekeeper it can be used for many wonderful purposes.

Bottom board: The bottom piece that makes up a standard hive. The hive boxes rest on top of it.

Brood: Any bee that is not fully developed including eggs, larvae and immature bees.

Brood chamber: The space where the queen is laying eggs and the rest of the brood is being tended to by nurse bees. Normally this will be found in the lower hive body and is somewhat spherically shaped.

Capped brood: Larvae cells that have a wax cover in place, once they have the wax cap, they spin their cocoon and turn into a pupa.

Cell: Hexagonally shaped spaces inside the comb. This is where the bees store honey and pollen as well as raise their brood.

Cleansing Flight: The first flight out of the hive to release built up bodily waste after an extended period of cold, during this cold confinement. The bees will not defecate in the hive and so will sometimes gain 50% of their body weight.

Cluster: Any mass of bees. Typically the queen will be found in the center of a cluster. These are found when bees swarm as well as when they are close together to combat cold weather.

Colony: A group of bees living together as one social unit.

Comb: Hexagonal cells that are built of beeswax. Set side by side and back to back to create a continuous, two sided wall of storage space and brood space.

Deep hive body: The standard large size box that uses full depth frames. This size box can also be used as super boxes.

Drone: The male honeybee.

Egg: The very first life stage of the honeybee. The queen lays eggs in the brood chamber.

Extractor: A hand or electric powered machine to spin honey out of the comb. It uses centrifugal force.

Food chamber: The space where the bees store their pollen and honey for future use. Can be found encircling the brood chamber and moving up from there.

Foulbrood: Bacterial diseases which affect the brood. Both American Foulbrood and European Foulbrood can be devastating to a colony although the American form is much more contagious. Treatment often includes destruction of the colony and the hive parts.

Frame: A narrow structure that fits inside the hive boxes and the supers. Used to support the wax comb and encourage the bees to build in a preplanned shape and design.

Hive: The home for your bees. Generally consists of two deep body boxes and various sized supers for honey collection.

Hive Tool: A metal tool shaped a bit like a flat crowbar. Used to work on the hives and pry apart stuck hive pieces.

Honeycomb: Wax comb that has been filled with honey and capped with wax.

Inner cover: A board that sits on top of the uppermost box of the hive. It has a ventilation hole to allow air into the hive and bees to leave via an upper exit. Has a small slot in the front edge that allows bees to leave.

Larva: The second stage of the honeybee. After the egg stage.

Laying worker: A worker bee that begins to lay eggs in the hive. Generally happens when a hive is without a queen. Their eggs are only capable of becoming drones because they are infertile.

Nosema disease: A digestive tract disease that causes various symptoms including disorientation. Can be treated and/or prevented with antibiotics. Can be debilitating to a colony.

Nucleus hive (Nuc): A small hive that is created to be used as a starter colony.

Outer cover: The top of the entire hive. This piece generally sits down atop the inner cover.

Package Bees: A "starter" set of bees that include several thousand worker bees and a queen. This is used to start a new colony.

Pollen: A fine powder that contains the microgametophytes of seed plants. Collected and used as a protein by the bees

Propolis: Resin collected by bees from plants and trees. This sticky resin is used to seal cracks in the hive and strengthen the comb.

Queen: The only fertile female bee in a colony. She lays all the eggs and is the literal mother of the entire colony.

Queenright: Term used to describe a colony which has a mated, actively laying queen.

Royal jelly: A glandular secretion that is used to feed all bees.

Smoker: A tool used by beekeepers to smoke the hive. It has a chamber where a smoldering fire is kept, a spout and a set of bellows that blows the smoke out the spout.

Stinger: A barbed needlelike piece of the bee's anatomy. This delivers the venom from the venom sac into the stung person. Typically tears away with the bee's abdomen after a sting.

Supercedure: The process by which a colony replaces an old or missing queen.

Swarm: A group of bees that have left their original hive with the old queen to escape an overcrowded situation.

Worker bee: The hive champion, the female honeybee does nearly all the work of the hive including protection duty, collecting food, raising young and cleaning to name just a few of her chores.

Index

R

Raccoons, 189
Rodents, 188

S

Sacbrood, 175
Salves, 194
Skunks, 189
slatted rack, 56
smoker, 66
splitting, 123, 162
Spring, 104
Stonebrood, 174
Strains of bees, 73
Summer, 123
super, 59
    adding, 119
swarm
    catching, 80

signs of, 114
swarming, 115, 121, 126, 127, 129, 130, 161
    prevent, 127

T

Terramycin, 151, 172

U

uncapping fork, 136
uncapping knife, 135

W

water source, 44
Wax Moth, 187
Winter, 156
winter cluster, 156
Worker, 29

18253213R10128

Made in the USA
Middletown, DE
27 February 2015